The Collected Works
Thoughts Aplenty
In Alphabetical Order

Marie Grace

Author of
The Mystery Mountain Collection
Volumes One, Two, Three and Four
Thoughts Aplenty

Thoughts Aplenty
The Collected Works in Alphabetical Order
Marie Grace
Author of The Mystery Mountain Collection: Volumes One, Two, Three and Four; and, Thoughts Aplenty

opyright © Marie Grace
2009

Published By Parables
November, 2017

All Rights Reserved. No part of this book may be reproduced or utilized in any form or by any means, electronic or mechanical, including photocopying, recording, or by any information storage and retrieval system, without permission in writing from the author.

Unless otherwise specified Scripture quotations are taken from the authorized version of the King James Bible.

    ISBN 978-1-945698-39-2
    Printed in the United States of America

Readers should be aware that Internet Web sites offered as citations and/or sources for further information may have been changed or disappeared between the time this was written and when it is read.

The Collected Works
Thoughts Aplenty
In Alphabetical Order

Marie Grace

Author of
The Mystery Mountain Collection
Volumes One, Two, Three and Four
Thoughts Aplenty

PUBLISHED by PARABLES
Earthly Stories with a Heavenly Meaning

MYSTERY MOUNTAIN ONE

Dedication

I dedicate this ***The Mystery Mountain Saga*** to my wonderful husband, David, and my friend and advisor

Jonathan Rainey. Also to my special friend, Janice Pratt.

My husband, David, has encouraged me from day one in the Saga Series, getting so excited sometimes as he read that he would shout out loud.

Jon has a Degree in Journalism, and been so kind as to proof read my manuscripts and inspire me to keep on going.

Janice is my confident, encourager, and company on my outings and book signings.

Thank you guys.
Marie Grace ☺

THOUGHTS APLENTY

Acknowledgment

I want to thank Dr. John Dee Jeffries for his care and help in republishing *Thoughts Aplenty*. Pastor Jeffries is the CEO/Acquisitions Editor of *Published By Parables*. He has also has been serving God's church as a pastor and preaching God's Word for over forty years.

Thank you, Pastor John, and I pray that God will bless you beyond your wildest dreams.

A Fan,
Marie Grace
☺

Table of Contents

Acknowledgement	3
Table of Contents	4
Preface	7
Introduction	11
A Guide for Making a Trip	13
A Phone Call (A short play/skit)	18
A Word of Comfort (A poem)	24
All-encompassing Prayer for Forgiveness	25
Alphameric (Numeric Value of Words)	27
America's National Anthem	28
(Star Spangled Banner)	28
Bible Books Tease (A crossword puzzle)	30
Big Kitty – A 25-pound Problem (Just for fun)	31
A Christian Nation (Our roots)	42
Conscientious Objector	48
Control Minimizing	51
Darwin's Deadly Descendants (Holocaust)	54
Discrimination	73
Dishwashers: Our Maids?	81
Eloise – My Terror-fleeing Friend	88
Fathers - Who Needs Them	94
Feelings	111
The Flag of the United States (A Tribute)	114

Hero-Trees (Sermon on the Mount and Fathers)	116
I feel Lousy (We all do sometimes)	122
Liberty (Does yours hurt someone else?)	123
Love Test (Do you really love your mate?)	127
My Prayer (Should be everyone's)	133
Ornaments of Easter (Keeping perspective)	134
Our God is an Awesome God (Just the facts)	140
Please Forgive My Hurt (Get rid of baggage)	144
Pyramid Schemes (Don't be sucked in)	153
Remember the Banana? (Especially teens)	159
Rewarding Bad Behavior (Don't teach kids rebellion)	170
Sailor Letter Home (Most powerful thing he's seen)	171
Singing the Psalms (Received comfort)	174
Single Scene (This WILL hurt)	182
Thoughts for the Day (The ultimate message)	198
Train up a child – "Butts" (Quit making excuses)	200
Try This (A prayer)	209
Unholy sex and sin (Biblical straight talk)	210
Volcanoes – Hell's Entrances? (Food for thought)	221
What color is your brain? (White or dark meat?)	230
You Are Responsible (A Warning)	243

THOUGHTS APLENTY

Preface

Thoughts Aplenty are my thoughts. You don't have to agree with me, but I sincerely hope that I challenge you to get into God's Word and see what the Bible really says – even if only to prove me wrong. Search and prove what I say for yourself so you will be a tree planted by the water, strong and unable to be moved.

Sometimes people don't like to sit down and read an entire book. Often-times they just do not have the time. Thoughts Aplenty is blunt, and without icing. Everything biblical can be verified in the Bible. Humor and profundity are also woven through this book to make readers laugh, think, and guess. Laughter is such good medicine.

After reading this book, you will probably love me or hate me. But remember, my heart and soul cry for the people who are being led down a wrong path of an unprepared, unready, and vulnerable soul…

DEATH IS FINAL, at that moment – you either go to Heaven or Hell.

Many churches no longer preach hell and damnation. If yours doesn't…get out of it. Find a church that is concerned for your everlasting soul, and teaches the whole word of God. I fear that many of these pastors and teachers are gently and kindly – so they won't offend anyone – letting their 'flocks' slip right into Hell!

God's never changes, neither does His Word!

I've been to what seemed like hell and back, and, like it or not, you need to hear truths. I'm a has-been smoker and drinker, a has-been rogue. I've been a corporate hatchet person, and I've wounded a lot of people.

To repeat myself, so my purpose for this book will eat into your thoughts, my heart now burns for souls and for people being led astray – oftentimes by well-meaning friends, pastors and teachers who just don't know what the Bible really teaches – or afraid to expound on truths. Don't be lulled into a false security. If you don't line up with God's Word, you are going to Hell!

If you are in a *cult* that teaches that abortion, homosexuality, pornography, child abuse, drinking, smoking, spouse abuse, taking the Lord's name in vain, divorce, violence, music so loud that no one can hear the Holy Spirit speak, and all other forms of malodorousness is alright, *run.* That is not God's church.

You cannot knowingly and purposely hurt someone else and be saved; you do not have the love of Christ in you.

My goal is not a popularity contest. My goal is to get *you* into God's Word – *the absolute authority* – so that Christ can save your soul from hell!

The Lord *Jesus* Christ is not willing that anyone should perish; neither am I.

The Lord had a big job with me to get me turned aground. I was probably one of His biggest challenges, but He was faithful and didn't give up - don't you either. God loves *YOU*…and don't you forget that. Come to Him just as you are, with all your baggage. He will help you through the cleanup process, just like He did with me. And if He was willing to clean up a creature like me…He will clean you up too.

Trust Him. He IS real!

THOUGHTS APLENTY

Introduction

Controversy will follow this book, and that is my idea. My prayer is that *Thoughts Aplenty* will make readers get into God's Word- the absolute authority.

Many myths are being perpetuated today, greasing the way to hell. Mind-numbed congregations are eating junk food and need to get back to critical thinking. I have written dialogs for sermonettes, plays and words of comfort. I've visited churches that don't even read from the Bible. I like visiting churches of various denominations when I am traveling. There is a vast difference in the churches. YOU are responsible to know that *your* church is teaching the real infallible God's Word.

Remember these words of wisdom…you can read a thousand books, and acquire lots of knowledge, *but* you have to study the Bible to learn *absolute truths!*

I totally know the tri-unity of God is real. Three beings in one. He's real, and it's wonderful. *Jesus IS* Lord!

When I start receiving a deep thought from Holy Spirit, I start typing just as the Spirit dictates. Many of my thoughts come very early in the morning or even during the night. When prayer is the last thing you do before you go to sleep at night, the connection with Our Lord is fresh in your mind, and He can speak to you…even in a dream.

I go back to the Bible to be sure that everything I have written lines up with God's Word, the absolute authority. I am sometimes amazed at how He gives me Scriptures that I may not have read for years. Our God is amazing!

I love giving in *secret*. I know if I get a reward here on earth, that is my reward. I'm trying to build rewards in Heaven. Where are *you* storing your rewards?

God and I have a few things we can laugh and rejoice about that we have partnered in over the decades. I love God's sense of humor…He's the one that created laughter. It's so good to laugh with Him…do *you* enjoy God…or are you such a sourpuss that a smile will crack your face? God and I have even played tricks (clean ones) on people during the years. He can be a riot! Do you have fun with God?

I urge everyone to make some secrets with God, and laugh with Him. Laughter is such good medicine. ☺ ☺

A Guide for Making a Trip to a Faraway Place

How many of you would like to take a trip to a faraway place? Let's see just how we would proceed making plans for a trip to this distant land. What would we take?

1. *Accommodations:* We would first want to know if there is going to be a place to stay.

    In my Father's house are many mansions…I go to prepare a place for you.
    John 14:2

First Class accommodations for us have been made in advance.

2. *Passports:* You can't travel without a passport.
    There shall in no wise enter into it anything that defileth… but they which are written in the Lambs' book of life.
    Revelation 21:27

Persons seeking entry will not be permitted past the *'gates'* without having proper credentials and having their name registered with the ruling authority.

3.   *Departure Times:* When do we leave?
   It is not for you to know the times or the seasons, which the Father hath put in His own power.
   Acts 1:7

The exact date of departure has not been announced. Travelers are advised to be prepared to leave on short notice.

4.   *Tickets:* What about our tickets?
   He that heareth My Word, and believeth on Him that sent Me, hath everlasting life, and shall not come into condemnation, but is passed from death into life.
   John 5:24

Your ticket is a written pledge that guarantees your journey. It should be claimed and its promises kept firmly in hand.

5.   *Customs:* How do we get through customs?
   If thou shalt confess with thy mouth the Lord *Jesus* and shalt believe in thine heart that God hath raised Him from the dead, thou shalt be saved.
   Romans 10:9

Only one declaration is required while going through customs.

6.   *Immigration:* What will our status be?
   They desire a better country, that is, an heavenly, for He hath prepared for them a city.
   Hebrews 11:16

All passengers are classified immigrants, since they are taking up permanent residence in a new country. The quota is unlimited.

7. *Luggage:* What will I take with me?
   We brought nothing into this world, and it is certain that we can carry nothing out.
   $$\text{1 Timothy 6:7}$$

No luggage or baggage whatsoever can be taken. No hair dryers, deodorants, money, cell phones, or the like of this world can go… just you alone!

8. Air Passage: What shall we watch for?
   We which are alive and remain shall be caught up together with them (the dead in Christ that rise first) in the clouds, to meet the Lord in the air; and so shall we ever be with The Lord.
   $$\text{1 Thessalonians 4:17}$$

Travelers going directly by air are advised to watch daily for indications of imminent departure.

9. *Vaccinations and inoculations:* I hate shots. What do we have to get?
   God shall wipe away all tears from their eyes; and there shall be no more death, nor sorrow, neither shall there be any more pain.
   $$\text{Revelation 21:4}$$

No injections of any kind will be needed, as diseases are unknown at this destination.

10. *Currency:* How much money and personal items shall I pack?
    Lay up for yourselves treasures in Heaven, where neither moth nor rust doth corrupt, and where thieves do not break through nor steal. Matthew 6:20

Supplies of treasures may be forwarded ahead to await the passenger's arrival.

Since you can't take it with you on the journey, advanced deposits should be as large as possible.

The only treasures you can forward are those you do for Christ.

11. *Clothing:* What kind of clothes should I pack?
    He hath clothed me with the garments of salvation.
    He hath covered me with the robe of righteousness.
    Isaiah 61:10

You will take nothing. A complete and appropriate new wardrobe is being provided for each traveler.

12. *Time Changes:* Will I have jet lag, or will my sense of time be off?
    The city has no need of the sun, neither of the moon, to shine in it; for the glory of God did lighten it, and the Lamb is the light thereof, there shall be no night.
    Revelation 21:23, 25

Resetting of watches will not be necessary to adjust to any day or night schedule.

13. *Reservations:* How do I get reservations?
    Now is the accepted time; behold, now is the day of salvation.
    2 Corinthians 6:2

Booking is now open. Apply at once.
TOMORROW MAY BE TOO LATE!!!

14. *Coronation Ceremony:* Who will meet me upon my arrival?

> There is laid up for me a crown of righteousness, which the Lord, the righteous judge, shall give me that day; and not to me only, but unto all them also that love His appearing.
> 2 Timothy 4:8

The highlight of the journey is when the Lord himself welcomes us at the reception and coronation, which awaits each new arrival.

And in the end – all we can take with us is someone else.

Where are we going?
              HEAVEN…

A Phone Call
A Play/Skit by Marie Grace

Moral: Things are not always as they seem.

Actors: Two ladies

Props: Two each, TV Trays or small tables, lamps, telephones

One each: Bible; romantic novel; young man's picture; new orange mop head (for wig); bubble gum

The scene opens with both ladies seated by end tables reading, in their own homes.

First Lady (#1) is on one side offstage, conservatively dressed with calf-length skirt and a buttoned-to-the-neck blouse, light makeup and neat hair. She is sitting in a chair and quietly and serenely reading her Bible, with the young man's picture – angled toward the audience – on the table beside her. A telephone is lying on the table.

Second Lady (#2) is sitting in a chair on the other side of the stage, dressed provocatively, lots of makeup, wearing a bright orange wig, and chewing bubble gum – stretching it in and out from her mouth and blowing bubbles as she reads the romance novel.

    She oohs and aahs and shrieks as she reads.

A few moments later, number two stops reading and looks at her watch. She wrinkles and wriggles her face, cheeks and lips around, obviously thinking about something serious.

After looking at the telephone on the table beside her several times during her *'thinking time'* she picks up the receiver and dials a number.

Lady #1's *telephone rings.* She looks at it a moment, then picks it up normally.

Lady #1: Hello

Lady #2 *(loud and brassy)*: "Yeah, uh, is Chris home?"

Lady #1: "No, may I take a message?"

Lady #1 sets her Bible down on the table and glances at the young man's picture.

Lady #2: "Nah, but I guess I should talk ta ya anyhows 'bout Chris's conduct."

Lady #2 sets her novel down on the table.

Lady #1 *(gasps and slaps her fingers over her mouth in surprise)*: "Chris's conduct?"

Lady #2 *(obviously annoyed)*: "Yea, man, ya perhaps needs ta talk ta Chris 'bout things goin' on."

(She stands up fast, fist to her hip. Her head becomes extended, with her chin out and slightly up.)

Lady #1 *(stammering, even more surprised)*: "Things going on?"

Lady #2 *(jerks chin in and tilts head a bit)*: "Yeah, man…"

Lady #1 *(obviously puzzled)*: "I'm sorry, I don't know what things you are speaking of."

Obviously irritated, Lady #2 starts mimicking Lady #1's correct speech by repeating – with lip service only – and chiding gestures toward the audience before she speaks again.

Lady #1 waits for Lady #2 to speak again, still looking puzzled.

Lady #2 *(her eyes rolling wide open in disbelief and her mouth hanging open as she continues)*: "Ya mean ya don't know w'at Chris and Judy are doin'?"

Lady #1 *(bewildered she sinks into the chair)*: "Uh, Judy? Judy… hmmm, I don't even know Judy."

Lady #2 *(throws her hand in the air and shakes her head, then sits back down)*: "A'm not su'prised, prob'ly keepin' 'er hid."

Lady #1 *(sits back up straight in with an indignant look in defense of Chris)*: "Hid? Chris has a very open relationship with us. We have complete trust in Chris."

Lady #2 goes back to silently mimicking the words of Lady #1, using weird facial expressions.)

Lady #2: "parently ya doesn't has as open a time as ya think – or ya'd know whet they're doin' 'hind yer back."

Lady #1 *(exhales very deeply with shock as she puts her hand over* her heart and slumps back into the chair and crosses her legs at her ankles):* "I just cannot believe Chris is doing anything behind our backs. Chris is such a good kid. At least tell me what you think they are doing."

Lady #2 *(now a bit snippy and curt with more mimicking gestures as she stands up again to speak):* "I s'pose ya think the smoke on Chris is jus' reg'lar smokes?"

Lady #1 *(gasps again with shock as she manages to sit up slightly to speak):* "I have never smelled smoke on Chris!"

Lady #2 *(holding the telephone away from her ear says to the audience):* "Dis Dame prob'ly don't know how to smell!"

As Lady #2's own comments crack her up, she laughs right out loud and slaps her knee, while adding into the telephone): "Wow, yur dummer'n I tho't!"

As Lady #1 sighs in utter disbelief, she can only stammer as she tries to speak – but her words are stuck in her throat): "I – what??"

Lady #2 *(just shakes her head back and forth, as she wiggles her face in a mimicking half-belief way as she almost looks sorry for Lady #1):* "Aye said yur dummer'n I tho't. I suppos' ya ain't even saw no dilated eyes or bruises on Chris's from drug needles. I'll bct ya don't even knows when yur bein' lied to…"

Lady #2 *(turns around and speaks directly to the audience):* "Lies are a good sign of drugs. Ya don't have to be smart or have a college education to watch yer kids for signs of drug use. It's all a matter of paying attention to them!"

Lady #1 *(responds emphatically as she totally collapses in her chair, with her legs and arms stretched out):* "Drugs? Never! I know my Chris has never touched drugs."

Lady #2 *(still facing the audience, her head slightly tipped sideways in an inquisitive manner, and her mouth hanging open again with her chin slightly protruded so audience can get her full expression as she continues):*" Lady, ya ain't very bright. Does ya even know what to look fo'? You, as a parent, needs to be informed, or you is just plain stupid!"

As she is trying to collect her composure, Lady #1 sits back up straight in her chair, crosses her legs at the ankles and picks up Chris's picture. As she is lovingly looking at the picture she is holding it so the audience can see the boy's face.

Lady #1: "I resent you implying my Chris is into anything immoral. I further resent you implying I am…I am…"

Lady #2 *(interrupts with a sharp tongue):* "Yo ignorance? Ya don't have to be dumb and ingnerant."

Lady#1 *(again cannot get her words out):* "I aah, I aah…"

Lady #2 *(interrupts Lady #1 again loudly):* "Hold it, I hear yur Chris commin' in now with my Tammie."

Lady #2 *(turns to face the side of the stage and shouts at an imaginary door):* "Christine, young lady, you get yo buns in here and talk to yo mama on the phone."

Lady #1 is obviously overwhelmed as she drops the telephone and collapses into her chair.

Lady #2 *(turns and faces the audience and asks them)*: "Do YOU *(emphasize)* know what to watch for?"

Lady #1 *(stands up and joins Lady #2 facing the audience as they both say together)*:

> LIES AND DRUGS GO TOGETHER…
> PAY ATTENTION!

The End.
Marie Grace

A Word of Comfort

God has happen what He sees fit,
And He has a reason for all of it.
Sometimes it is hard to understand,
But He knows best from beginning to end.

When the heartaches and evils of life befall you,
Remember this: it has others too.
God knows that for us to be strong,
We must learn the difference between right and wrong.

There is but one way to accomplish this,
And not much of it can be called bliss.
But if things were soft and not like steel,
There would be no reason for Heaven or Hell.

A fully content mind is but a lazy mind,
You would need nothing, so nothing you'd find.
But just as long as you want and need,
God's great words you'll continue to heed.

By Marie Grace when she was only 14 years old for a neighbor who just lost her husband.

All-encompassing Prayer for Forgiveness

Merciful Lord *Jesus*, maker of Heaven and Earth, my Redeemer, please hear my cry.

With a humble and contrite heart, I confess all of my sins of this very day, this week, this year and all of the sins of my entire life.

The sins of omission and of commission; the sins of my morose, perversely obstinate, and angry temper; sins of life, love, lip, and walk; of hard-heartedness and unbelief; of presumption and pride; of unfaithfulness to the souls of men; sins of a lack of boldness in the decisions for the cause of Christ; sins of deficiency and out-spoken zeal for Your glory; sins of bringing dishonor upon Your great name.

I confess my sins of deception to you and to others, sins of injustice, untruthfulness in my dealings with others; sins of impurity in my thoughts, words, and deeds; of covetousness; sins of substance, unduly hoarded, squandered, not consecrated to your glory; sins in private and in the family; sins in my study and recreation; sins in the study of your Word, and the lack of it, of trying to make it fit my desires instead of yours, and the neglect of it; sins in prayer irreverently offered and in cold withheld.

Sins in time misspent, sins in yielding to Satan's wiles, in opening my heart to his temptations and corruptions; the sin of obsession with or affinity for evil; sins of being unwatchful when I knew Satan was near; sins of quenching Holy Spirit; sins against light and knowledge; sins against conscience and the restraints of Holy Spirit; sins against your love; and sins of not heeding the still, gentle voice of Holy Spirit when He was speaking to me.

I hereby confess all my sins, known and unknown, felt and unfelt, confessed and not confessed, remembered or forgotten, knowing, good Lord, that you forgive, and with my sincere prayers you will put all of my sins in your Sea of Forgetfulness, never to be remembered again. Please Lord, I ask that you wash me completely with your precious blood and wrap your healing and protective stripes around me to keep me safe from the enemy greater than me, but not greater than You.

Help me, oh Lord, to be what you want me to be. Give me your sweet Holy Spirit to guide me and the courage to listen to Him.

Please come into my heart and dwell forever.

I acknowledge and believe that The Lord *Jesus* Christ came to earth, was nailed to a tree, died an agonizing death to shed his precious blood for my every need.

I believe that He raised from the dead on the third day by his Father, Almighty God. He ascended into Heaven, where He is waiting for me to join Him at either my death or the Resurrection of my body when He comes back for His Own.

I pray in the Name above all Names, *Jesus* Christ.

Alphameric

A = 1		J = 10		S = 19

B = 2		K = 11		T = 20

C = 3		L = 12		U = 21

D = 4		M = 13		V = 22

E = 5		N = 14		W = 23

F = 6		O = 15		X = 24

G = 7		P = 16		Y = 25

H = 8		Q = 17		Z = 26

I = 9		R = 18

K N O W L E D G E
11+14+15+23+12+5+4+7+5 - equals 96 percent

H A R D W O R K
8+1+18+4+23+15+18+11 – equals 98 percent

A T T I T U D E
1+20+20+9+20+21+4+5 – equals 100%

America's National Anthem

I

Oh, say can you see, by the dawn's early light,
What so proudly we hailed at the twilight's last gleaming?
Whose broad stripes and bright stars
through the perilous fight,
O'er the ramparts we watched were so gallantly streaming?
And the rockets' red glare, the bombs bursting in air,
Gave proof through the night that our flag was still there.
O say does that star-spangled banner yet wave
O'er the land of the free and the home of the brave?

II

On the shore dimly seen through the mists of the deep,
Where the foe's haughty hosts in dread silence reposes,
What is that which the breeze, o'er the towering steep,
As it fitfully blows, half concealed, half discloses?
Now it catches the gleam of the morning's first beam,
In full glory reflected now shines in the stream,
Tis the star-spangled banner! O long may it wave
O'er the land of the free and the home of the brave!

III

And where is that band who so vauntingly swore,
That the havoc of war and the battle's confusion
A home and a Country should leave no more?
Their blood has washed out their foul footsteps' pollution.
No refuge could save the hireling and slave
From the terror of flight, or the gloom of the grave,
And the star-spangled banner in triumph doth wave
O're the land of the free and the home of the brave.

Written by Francis Scott Key of Georgetown, Maryland, September 3-14, 1814, and designated as the National Anthem of America by an Act of Congress, March 3, 1931.

NOTE:
If you don't know this, memorize it and teach it to your children!

Bible Books Tease

L	E	V	I	T	I	C	U	S	S	E	L	C	I	N	O	R	H	C
A	M	O	L	F	I	R	S	T	K	I	N	G	S	O	M	A	R	F
M	A	S	S	I	S	E	N	E	G	O	B	A	D	I	A	H	I	C
E	L	N	F	I	R	S	T	T	I	M	O	T	H	Y	T	R	O	I
N	A	A	C	T	S	A	M	T	A	U	H	S	O	J	S	N	L	A
T	C	I	R	O	N	I	A	K	R	E	D	U	J	T	D	L	H	C
A	H	H	P	S	A	L	M	S	R	U	T	O	S	T	I	A	O	E
T	I	T	U	S	E	K	U	K	K	A	B	A	H	P	N	R	S	A
I	S	N	A	V	H	A	I	A	S	I	M	E	I	O	I	I	I	E
O	B	I	E	Z	R	A	D	E	U	U	S	A	J	N	A	R	C	O
N	O	R	L	E	R	J	A	M	E	S	N	E	T	N	A	O	S	E
S	R	O	E	S	S	O	P	L	A	S	T	H	S	H	N	O	A	R
L	E	C	I	T	H	E	V	L	N	N	I	S	C	D	A	Y	O	L
E	T	D	K	H	E	L	O	A	H	A	E	E	K	A	M	N	A	H

Genesis, Exodus, Leviticus, Numbers, Deuteronomy, Joshua, Judges, Ruth, First Samuel, Second Samuel, First Kings, Second Kings, First Chronicles, Second Chronicles, Ezra, Nehemiah, Esther, Job, Psalms, Proverbs, Ecclesiastes, Song of Solomon, Isaiah, Jeremiah, Lamentations, Ezekiel, Daniel, Hosea, Joel, Amos, Obadiah, Jonah, Micah, Nahum, Habakkuk, Zephaniah, Haggai, Zechariah, Malachi, Matthew, Mark, Luke, John, Acts, Romans, First Corinthians, Second Corinthians, Galations, Ephesians, Philippians, Colossians, First Thessalonians, Second Thessalonians, First Timothy, Second Timothy, Titus, Philemon, Hebrews, (James), First Peter, Second Peter, First John, Second John, Third John, Jude, Revelation.

Big Kitty: A 25-pound Rascal
(Just a story to make you smile)

I'm allergic to animals, including cats, but I can tolerate poodles. So, we had a toy poodle for about fifteen years. She was literally my 'baby' and went everywhere with me. When I lost Missey Sue Mutley it broke my heart. Everyone kept saying I needed to get another animal, but just couldn't. How do you replace a *'kid'* with another one? I still find it hard to talk about her without crying. For fifteen years she was my constant companion.

I've rescued many animals in past years, and I've spent a fortune taking them to a vet, getting their health checked out and all needed vaccinations. Then I would adopt them out…always checking out the new 'parents'…

It's almost been a hobby, and even people around the neighborhood know that I take injured, lost, and dumped dogs and cats. One good friend of mine who lives on the next block from me brought me two newborn baby kittens she found in the dumpster. I stayed up night and day for the first few days to keep them warm and feed them. They became beautiful kittens and eventually were adopted out together.

People who abuse animals are real creeps, and someone putting newborn animals in a dumpster is a hideous creature. I hope God Almighty dumpsters them.

Anyway, I just could not bring myself to get another pet. I would just get by with helping the abused ones.

Missey Sue had a pet door in the laundry room, and I never had the courage to close it up. It just seemed like it needed to remain open.

One afternoon I had just finished emptying the dishwasher and was wiping down the sink. All of a sudden, I hear this big '*Rooaaarr*' behind me. It scared me so much that I almost jumped into the sink. When I turned around, I saw this big, long soft haired golden-honey-orange Persian monster with big very gold eyes. His neck was crooked, and his head was tilted sideways. I had never seen such a big cat before. He kept on talking to me until I realized I really wasn't under attack.

When I reached down to pet him, he started his big motor, sort of like a 10-cylinder. His ears were dark inside with gunk, and he was filthy.

I called my vet's office at Glenfair and they got us right in. I dug out Missey Sue's pretty brocade pet carrier. Talk about a job – getting this big gold monster into a carrier meant for a 12-pound poodle. I kept praying for God not to let this creature bite me. But the cat seemed to know I was trying to help him. He sure didn't want to be in the little pet carrier, but all he did was to complain… loudly and constantly.

He was frightened in the truck as I drove. He was shaking and trembling so badly that it made my GMC truck move. He actually looked relieved when I took him out of my truck and into the vet's office.

The doctor checked him out…and he was complaining all the time. We got to laughing at how vocal he was.

The gunk in his ears was not mites, as I had suspected, so the doctor cleaned them out really good and put medicine in them. He weighed him in at 25-pounds and 4-ounces. I understand that the average cat weighs between 6 and 12 pounds. I also had the vet give him all the vaccinations, including rabies and feline leukemia, that he could possibly need. Big Kitty had been neutered, and his front claws removed. The doctor figured he had been thrown out of a moving vehicle. Sadly, he had seen this type of injury before. Sure explained why he was trembling so much in my truck. I'll bet he figured he'd be air-bound again shortly.

The doctor took x-rays of his neck and back, and couldn't see anything broken. He felt that physical therapy would straighten his neck up. The doctor prescribed more of the medicine to put in Big Kitty's ears twice a day for ten days. He felt the cat was about 18-month to two years old.

So, it would be a while before he could be adopted out. I would be stuck with him for at least three weeks just for physical therapy. The vet also said that if he didn't already have several cats he would take Big Kitty because of his wonderful nature. Big Kitty let the vet, and me, do anything to him we wanted to, and he did nothing but jaw…all the time running his ten-cylinder as he vocalized...making him really funny to listen to.

I kid you not…putting medicine in a 25+ pound cat's ears twice a day is no easy task, along with giving him a syringe of antibiotic in his cheek. I had to catch Big Kitty when he wasn't looking...he had gotten on to me…and would run out the pet door and hide. I'd get him between my knees, with my feet crossed so he couldn't back-out. Sometimes he seemed to be made of pliable rubber. He did not like being medicated.

But we survived, and his ears cleared up. But his neck was still somewhat crooked. The rest of his life he drank liquids with his head tilted sideways. His face would get all wet. He must have decided he liked for his face and whiskers to get wet so he could come in and jump up on my lap to get toweled off, getting me all wet in the process. Big Kitty loved attention.

I cannot stand the smell of a cat litter box. It is putrid to me. But guess what? Big Kitty always went outside to do his business. Never once in all the years he was with me did he make one single mess in the house. No marking furniture…

I had never intended to keep this amazing animal…that's why I never named him anything…but Big Kitty.

God is cognizant of our every need. In my own strength, I was not able to accept a replacement for Missey Sue. My caring Heavenly Father knew that a cat wouldn't be in competition with Missey Sue's memory. And the fact that the cat was injured meant I would take care of him. He knew I would grow to love Big Kitty… and I did.

He had so much personality, and lots of hair. I had to comb Big Kitty every day, and he loved it. All I had to do was pick up the brush, and he was up in my lap. Do you have any idea how it feels to have a 25-pound creature jump up into your lap? Bid Kitty was more affectionate than any feline critter I had ever seen. But man, that cat sure talked a lot – and loudly. It was like he was actually carrying on a conversation with me.

I had ceramic tile in my kitchen, dining-room and hallway.

I kept a runner in the hallway. There was a linen closet at the end of the hall – a straight shot… He would take a running leap and jump on the end of the runner and slide clear down the hall – hitting the linen closet door with a 'bang.' I was always sure I could see a smug grin on his face as he walked back by me. With twenty-five pounds on the move, hitting an immovable object – it could raise a person right up out of their seat, especially the first time someone heard it.

Big Kitty could not handle change. He didn't like the furniture moved. I had my bedroom and living-room carpets replaced one year. My bedroom was at the back of the house. Big Kitty was out somewhere prowling when the furniture and old carpeting were taken out of the bedroom. I didn't see him come in just as the two gentlemen were putting down the new carpet and pad. The men were laughing and talking, but stopped suddenly. I didn't think anything about it. The quiet continued for several minutes. Finally, I walked back to look in the door and see if everything was alright. Both men were huddled in the far corner…looking terrified. Standing by me in the doorway was this vocalizing cat watching them.

A terrified voice whispered to me, "Is he going to attack us?"

I looked down at this jawing feline…and I swear he was sneering with a silly grin.

I assured them that they were not under attack, and Big Kitty was just filled with curiosity. I picked up the golden ball of fur and took him over to the men to get *'acquainted'*…they were fine after that. They said later that they had never heard a cat actually carrying on a non-stop conversation. He was definitely gabby.

They finished the bedroom, and then it was time for the living room. As they started moving the furniture out to the front stoop, here came the cat. Big Kitty actually wrapped his front paws around the legs and hung onto each piece of furniture to stop it from being moved as they picked it up. I had never seen an animal act like that; neither had the gentlemen. They kept cracking up now that they knew they were in no danger.

If Big Kitty decided he wanted our attention, he would even grab a hold of one of our legs with his front paws and hang on, forcing us to drag him with us until we paid some attention to him. Have you ever tried to walk with twenty-five plus pounds of dead weight attached to a leg? Or, if I was not expecting him to jump up in my lap – and I was suddenly pounced on – I did pay attention to him.

He was a real jewel. He did have one really bad habit. He was fascinated with my telephone answering/fax machine. I had to be sure and close my office door when I wasn't in my office. If I forgot, he would run out all of the tape, retrieving my messages. He would call people with the programmed buttons. He loved to push the red button for monitoring. He loved to hear the, *'Beep, beep, beep', if you would like to make a call, please hang up the telephone and try again."* He thought the operator was actually talking to him. I told people if they left a message and I didn't get back with them, to please call again – because Big Kitty probably took the call.

Big Kitty would get up on my desk, and if I wasn't watching him, stretch out, and knock everything off onto the floor…as he watched with a grin. Then he would 'help' me pick up and sort everything – Play time…

I had notes posted on the side of my metal file cabinet, attached with small, cute magnet characters. When I wasn't looking, he would take his front paws and feverishly pull them all down.

Then I would get to pick up, sort and rehang again. All to his jawing at me – amidst smiles of *'ha, ha's'*.

I walked into my office and found the receiver off the hook. Big Kitty was lying there on my now empty desk, looking innocent. I didn't think too much about it until the phone rang immediately after I hung it up. It was my Spiritual daughter, Theresa. She was very worried. Her telephone had rung; but when she picked up the receiver, no one was there. She checked the *caller ID* and it said the call came from my number. Theresa tried to call back, but the line was busy. She was about to come down to see what was going on when she finally got through.

Yep…Big Kitty had made another phone call. He punches the automatic dial numbers I have programmed on my machine, after he slides his paw under the receiver to knock it out of the cradle.

This wasn't the first time he had made a phone call.

He was sure a silly polecat.

He loved dogs. He must have grown up with them. Our neighbor, John, had three dogs he liked to take for walks each morning on leashes. Big Kitty would watch for them, run out, and rub against the dogs, and dart in and out between the larger Lab, Lady's, legs, almost tripping her. I was always amazed that the big black Lab tolerated this obnoxious feline.

The cat was a lot larger than the small dog, Daiscy, and Big Kitty would often knock her right off her feet trying to rub against her to love her. Daisey would look up at John as if to say, "Help."

Lucky was a Terrier mix, and very young and lively, and he seemed to enjoy Big Kitty's attention. They would jump at each other like they were going to attack, then change directions to avoid a collision.

Big Kitty slept on his back quite often, with his paws up in the air. And while he was sleeping he was constantly making air-biscuits. Boy did he like a quick belly-rub when we walked by.

We had lazy Boy recliners we liked to relax in, where we would watch the news at night. One evening, we were reposed and winding down our busy days, when in marches Big Kitty with something in his mouth. He headed straight for *'daddy'* as the little creature was making all sorts of screaming sounds. Big Kitty gently laid his little object down at my husband's feet, looked up at him and seemed to say, "This little guy has a problem, fix it." My husband picked up the little bird. It didn't have a feather ruffled. Instead of killing the little bird, he had brought it to Daddy to put back up in its nest…so daddy did.

A few years ago, when our grandson was only two years old, he and I had been shopping. We stopped by my home to drop off my items before heading to his house. Zack loved Big Kitty, but he runs outside every time my grandson comes over, because Zack always wants to pick him up.

As I walked in, the phone was ringing, so I put my load on the counter and reached for it. Zack had spotted Big Kitty and the chase was on. The phone call was a wrong number, so I hung up. I turned around as I heard a muffled sound, "Grandma, open the door. Grandma, please open the door?" It sounded like my grandson had gotten outside. I didn't know how; all the doors were shut and locked. I ran to the utility room (I had no pool) where the pet door was – to see what was going on. (It only takes 2 seconds for a child to get in harm's way.)

There he was, his little bottom sticking out the pet door, on the utility room side, and his head out of sight on the others side of the door. I ran out the back door to the utility room door where he could see me. I knew if he could see me there would be less chance that he would panic. He wasn't upset at all. I wanted to run for the camera, but I didn't want him to feel alone, so the visualization of Zack stuck in the doggie door is just a memory in my mind.

He told me again to open the door (utility room).

I twisted his little body sideways as I talked to him and he slipped right on out. I was so proud to realize he, at two years old, was looking for a way to correct the situation, and not succumbing to the 'victim mentality'… He reasoned that if the door was opened he could get out, that he wasn't really in danger. He didn't try the doggie door again.

Big Kitty seemed to have that smirk on his face again as he watched the proceedings, but at one point, in his verbalizing…I thought I heard him giggle.

Sadly, I lost my Polecat Buddy about three years ago. His kidneys shut down.

About a year-and-a-half ago, I became aware of another little puppy. He is a Chihuahua. Someone had found him out in a field, alone and very emaciated. He was only about 6 weeks old. They didn't know if he had any siblings that had been 'dropped' off out in the country. If so, he was the only one who had survived.

Getting very hungry, and not knowing any better, he had eaten rocks. The Humane Society Veterinarian Clinic had done bowel surgery on him, and had saved his life. I saw him on the Net, and fell in love with the little guy. They were calling him Shep. He needed more healthcare, and probably wasn't going to be adoptable. For a beginner, he had two complete sets of teeth in his little mouth. The Vet couldn't explain why. But he would have to be a little older, like six months, before they could remove them.

Well, a little guy in need??? That's all I needed to adopt him. I added 'pie' to Shep, calling him *'Sheppie'*. The surgery for his teeth removal was done when he was about six months old. I didn't know anything about Chihuahua's…It was a learning experience. They really are *'ankle biters'* as they are so appropriately called. Everyone said I would have a hard time training him to go out to 'potty' because they are hard to train.

WRONG…We picked him up about seven on a Wednesday evening, and I took him outside a couple of times that night, and once during the night…and by Thursday, the next morning, he was going out on his own. He has never made a mess in the house. He is very loyal. His biggest problem is his big mouth…but that means he is a great watch dog. It's funny how he does not bark during the night if he hears something. Instead, he lowers his voice and tries growling a deep growl…probably to make anything threatening outside think he is a German Shepherd.

Pets are good for us. They give older people a reason to get up in the mornings, they have someone to care for, that depends on them. In getting a pet for an older person, however, MAKE SURE the pet doesn't require more care than the elderly person is able to give. Also, be sure if your loved one is in a *'care center'* that they allow pets, and have the areas for them to do their duty. You can't just give a pet to someone with good wishes. You have to be practical, and think about such things as care and responsibility.

I don't think a pet should ever be given to a youngster incapable of taking care of the pet. Nor do I think you should ever allow your child – of any age - to abuse a family pet. I've seen this happen, and it's tragic. Don't let your little one carry the pet around by the neck or tail. This is cruelty. Don't ever let your little one bite the dog or the cat. I've seen stupid parents punish pets because they responded to being bitten or hit with a toy. Sometimes I think the parents need to be bitten to wake them up – and make them think.

Think what you are doing!

People who abuse animals are idiots!

A Christian Nation

The Supreme Court Decision, 1892, Church of the Holy Trinity VS the United States.

> Our laws and our institutions must necessarily be based upon and embody the teachings of ***The Redeemer*** of mankind. It is impossible that it should be otherwise; and in this sense and to this extent our civilization and our institutions are emphatically Christian…This is a Religious people. This is historically true. From the discovery of this continent to the present hour, there is a single voice making this affirmation…we find everywhere a clear recognition of the same truth…These, and many other matters which might be noticed, add volume of unofficial declarations to the mass of organic utterances that this is a Christian nation.

Our Founding Fathers in no way excluded the Judeo-Christian influence from any portion of either Politics or Government. On the contrary, our Founding Fathers relied upon Biblical principles in creating the United States of America. The United States Constitution they wrote guarantees freedom FOR religion – not freedom FROM religion.

The phrase so many quote, "A wall of separation' between church and state" is not in the Constitution. That statement was made by Thomas Jefferson ***15 years after*** the Constitution was written. Actually, Thomas Jefferson had ***nothing*** to do with the making of our United States Constitution. It was written while he was away in Paris as the United States' minister to France.

The phrase ***wall of separation,*** indicating an impassable gulf – is nowhere in our Constitution. Even the phrase ***church and state*** is not found in the United States Constitution, specifically in the First Amendment.

This phrase has its origins taken out of context, and outright misquoting Jefferson, by people bent on destroying this Nation. In the letter written by Thomas Jefferson in 1802, he was writing to a group of Baptists and Congregationalists in Danbury, Connecticut, in response to ***their question*** regarding Jefferson's PERSONAL opinion of the actual meaning of the First Amendment. IT HAD ABSOLUTELY NOTHHING TO DO WITH THE FORMING OF THE UNITED STATES CONSTITUTION'S FIRST AMENDMENT!

This was Jefferson response – to the Baptists and Congregationalists - that the "wall of separation between Church and State" – "It is a matter of religion." Which he reiterated in 1805 in his second Inaugural Address. It was not to Congress…it was to the Church. It had, and has, nothing to do with the Constitution of the United States.

This shows how evil has infiltrated into our Society. The only thing needed for evil to flourish – is for good people to do nothing. What are YOU doing?

The Founding Fathers NEVER intended a separation of God from government. Nor did they ever intend for there to ever be a separation of religious people from involvement in politics and government.

The First Amendment was and is to guarantee that the powers of the government are to be limited, and would never be used to establish one church or denomination over another. The Amendment was to completely keep the government OUT of religion, and to not be able to make any Laws curtailing people's religious beliefs.

In other words, the federal government should never interfere with matters of religion. That must always be left up to the people – AND GOD.

George Washington wrote, "The adoption of the Constitution will demonstrate as visibly the finger of Providence (GOD) as any possible event in the course of human affairs can ever designate it."

The very FIRST Amendment to our United States Constitution was about religious freedom…think about that! It says:

> ***"Congress shall make no laws respecting an establishment of religion, or prohibiting the free exercise thereof; or abridging the freedom of speech, or of the press; or the right of the people PEACEFULLY to assemble, and to petition the Government for a redress of grievances."***

I call your attention to one word – **_PEACEFULLY_** – that means that the riots we have been witnessing are NOT protected by the Constitution…It's as plain as day.

Plus, we have these nincompoops who way 'Christians should not be involved in politics…' Webster's defines these nut jobs as 'Simpletons' and fools.

All through the Bible, the real one, in both the Old Testament and the New Testament, GOD gave people many instructions to be involved in government politics. Take Moses, David, Solomon, Daniel, and many kings. They were GOD's messengers in government and politics. What do you naysayers do with this? I've listed a few Biblical directives GOD gave to Christians:

1) Participate in running the government; Luke 19:13.

2) Do what is necessary to improve the community; Nehemiah 2:17-18.

This was another city where GOD commanded them to build a wall, and restore government. So, they strengthened their hands to do good. God had almost all of the nations He established build walls for protection.

3) Seek justice; Isaiah 1:17. We, as followers of God, are to seek justice for the oppressed, the widowed, and the fatherless. Is not this controlling government? Are not these political actions? I'm sure you can add many more commandments from GOD Himself about us being involved in politics and keeping government in Christian restraints.

America is in a sad state of affairs because, for the most part, Christians have sat on their tushes during Elections. Voting for someone because of a certain Party, and not even knowing what that person stands for is being a partaker in their evil…

Do you realize if YOU vote for a person who supports abortion – you are a partaker in the evil of murdering babies? God said HE knew each one of those little ones FROM THE MOMENT OF CONCEPTION. It is a baby from inception…why are Christians allowing ungodly people to debate when life begins? If during an

Election, YOU don't vote, like the more than 20 million Christian don't...YOU are a partaker in evil! To not do something you should...is the same as voting for the evil that is ensnaring this great country. To not vote...is doing Satan's work for him.

Psalms 55:15 - is a good example of what God demands of everyone who promotes evil. *"Let death seize upon them, and let them go down quick into Hell: for wickedness is in their dwellings, and among them."* Does this sound like God overlooks people that participate in, or allow evil to flourish? No, Christians are to combat evil.

Luke 19:13b – *Jesus* Himself speaking. *"Occupy til I come."* He was referring to the true Christians to take command, discharge and control over what happens on earth until He returns. Webster's Dictionary explain 'occupy' as "To take hold of, to grab or seize and control as the owner." Almighty God owns this earth, and as his children we are to do His bidding, and keep control of HIS earth until He returns.

Those two verses sure debunk the false teaching that we, as Christians, are to not get involved in politics and government affairs.

I have personally heard David Barton and William J. Federer speak. I've acquired several of their truly enlightening books. Both men are more familiar with our actual and true United States of America's beginnings than anyone else I have ever studied. It would be expedient for every person, especially Christians, to read, hear and watch anything they can read, hear, see or study these two well informed men have to say. I must warn you, however, you have to listen really fast...That's why I have purchased so many of their books...I cannot listen that fast. ☺ ☺

They are both deliberate and accurate. They will give you and yours the ammunition you need to reject and correct this runaway society. A society of liberals, often actual Communists, brainwashing our children with their revision of history. They are even deleting patriotic words from our dictionaries.

I'm a big proponent of mandatory family meetings. They are imperative for a strong and united family. Both Barton and Federer's works, especially their videos, would be a good way to start mandatory meetings – especially including DAD! God says the dad is the one who is responsible for his family, not only for substance, but for education.

I sound like an infomercial for these two men, but I'm not. I have just listened and watched both so often that I really deem them both as Constitutional Historians. Both very well informed in most Supreme Court decisions, which they often quote.

HOW LONG HAS IT BEEN SINCE YOU HAVE READ THE UNITED STATES CONSTITUTION IN ITS ENTIRETY? IT DOESN'T TAKE THAT LONG, AND SHOULD BE READ BY EVERY AMERICAN AT LEAST ONCE EVERY THIRD YEAR. IT SHOULD, AND MUST, BE READ TO OUR CHILDREN. THEY WILL NOT LEARN IT IN SCHOOL.

Conscientious Objector

It is with a great sorrow in my heart when I hear believers, and even from some pulpits, saying total nonviolence is the correct way to live. I do not believe that this is what the real Bible teaches at all. The belief just pushes Christians on down the road to a conciliatory frame of mind and destruction, ready for the antichrist.

Our Lord *Jesus* physically threw thieves, corrupt merchants, and moneychangers out of His temple with a whip. He was not a pacifist! To me, this positively shows us that this total nonsense of nonviolence rhetoric being pumped into our heads to control us is not at all biblical. It is not one of Christ's teachings, but man'.

An even more specific lesson is in Luke, chapter 23, and verse 36 where it says, "Then said He unto them, but now, he that hath a purse, let him take it, and likewise his scrip: and he that *hath no sword,* let him sell his garment, and buy one." This is not to say we should be warmongers, because we should not! Blessed are the peacemakers. But we are to be on guard for evil attacks. We are to strengthen and protect other Christians, especially the weaker ones, but we cannot if we are weak and unprepared ourselves. We must be ready, physically and spiritually, to stand firm against whatever comes our way. I do not believe there is a single Scripture in either the Old or New Testaments to support the concept that a *'good'* God enjoins pacifism on anyone.

Exodus 17:16, says even the Lord makes war.

Numbers 11:3, God set the age that men must go to war, twenty years and up. This was to verify that we people of God are to go to physical and spiritual war. In fact, a lot of Numbers is telling God's people that they must go to war…to make wrong right.

Numbers 10:9, "And if you go to war in your land against an enemy who oppresses you, the Lord God will remember you." We are to fight for our Nation, our people and our land. It is the honorable thing to do.

Deuteronomy 1:41, If you do not go to war, you allow your children to be prey. God calls that SIN.

The Bible is full of verses that say we are to stand up against evil, and protect our families and our country. So, for anyone to say Christians should not get involved in either war or controlling the government…God says they are sinners if they don't.

Paul even uses the analogy of faithful service in the army as a model of Christian commitment in 2 Timothy 2:4, A soldier must have one thing on his mind - to carry out his duty; the Christian must also have the same goals and consecrations…to please Christ *Jesus* – not man.

The Militia is not the National Guard, nor the Air Force, nor the Army, nor the Marine Corps, nor the Navy; it is the people, the whole people *except for a few public officials*. The idea of a nation in arms is not revolutionary – it is biblical. We are to protect our families, our friends, and our country. If the people are disarmed, we become victims of any evil force wanting power. That's how dictators get to power, by disarming the good people.

The great apostle, Paul, in his 1 Timothy Epistle, chapter 5, verse 4, commands instruction, training and teaching at home, making it the responsibility of the parents, not the church, to teach the real Bible to their children and grandchildren. (In the Greek text, the word nephew used here really means grandchildren.) This means it is the parents responsibility to teach their children to take care of their families and their country.

Verse 8 continues with the fact that if anyone does not provide for his/her own, they are not of the faith, and they are worse than infidels. This means all aspects of their family's needs, from the love of God, to the physical protection.

As Americans and Christians, we are to protect, support, and defend each other. We are not to become disarmed and victims whose constitutional freedoms will be stripped away because of cowardliness.

GOD wiped out entire nations because of evil. Including their animals. God fights evil…and so should we.

We should ALL be recognizing and honoring - and fully supporting – our men and women who, as part of our American family, are doing their honorable service to God and to us.

Control Minimizing

What to do when your ex-spouse drops off the kids and wants to give you a hard time, and a two-hour lecture on what the kids can and cannot do.

First: Your ex-spouse (or you) have unresolved anger. Drop-off time is NOT the time or place for either of you to vent anger. *It should never be done in front of the kids!* That is a totally selfish act for either one of you, and such a terrible example of how badly adults who put themselves before their little ones behave. A life-marking act for them to witness because of your or your ex-spouse's bad behavior.

The moment your ex-spouse arrives with the kids, greet him/her *cheerfully* at the door. They do not need to come inside. Tell him/her quickly and politely to type up a list of what they say the kids can or cannot do, and you'll post it conspicuously. If you cannot get a word in edgewise, just hand him/her a not stating that. Then go to the bathroom and lock the door. Do not stay and argue with him/her. Don't wait for a response! ***ARGUMENT IS THE EXCHANGE OF IGNORANCE!!!***

Second: The next time your kids are dropped off, and the ex wants to argue and/or be the 'Big Cheese" just politely but firmly say, "The rules are posted!" Then shut the door.
Don't wait for a response. Argument will give your ex the upper hand.

In my opinion, long lectures are to make the delivering ex-spouse look like a dog in front of the kids. To make you look insufficient, stupid and foolish. Don't feed their need to control you. Don't give anyone else the upper hand. Don't fall for it. Do not fall into a trap that will just keep getting worse and your ex-spouse gains more and more of the upper-hand. Always remember; *ARGUMENT IS THE EXCHANGE OF IGNORANCE.* Do not fall into the trap. State your ONE-LINE fact, then leave (shut the door) without waiting for a response. If you respond, he/she has got you.

I have found that when someone has to write down something, he/she usually uses a lot fewer words. This puts you in peaceful control. Without argument, you have control of the shut-off valve. This will make you look good in front of the kids. If your spouse forces him/herself into your home…call the Police. You will not have to do it more than once.

Example: When our daughter was a teenager, we posted the 'House Rules' on her bedroom door. All who entered read them, and I never had to say a word to anyone. We enjoyed our daughter's teen years, and her friends all liked to be at our home.

Now, this will also work when you are picking up the kids. Go up to the door, but do not go inside. If you do – you are in their territory and the underling. Ask for the kids to come out to the car; then go back to the car. If he/she follows you out to the car, roll up the windows and turn the radio on while you are waiting. You can have a paper already written out with your rules or asking for his/her written rules. Tape it to the window so he/she cannot see your face, only the letter. This takes power away from them and gives you peaceful control.

Don't want or expect a response, or you will give them back the control

Usually those on the receiving end are on the defensive and want to justify themselves. You don't have to justify yourself to anyone but GOD!

Kids belong in the backseat with their seatbelts fastened. So only unlock one back door for them to get in. Leave as soon as the kids are correctly fastened in their seatbelts. (IF you love your kids, you will have them in seatbelts!)

If you allow your child to ride in the front seat, especially one that is being fed misconceptions, it will give them a certain power over you.

If your ex tries to block the car from leaving, peacefully and quietly call 911. After only one police call, they won't try that again.

REMEMBER; ARGUMENT IS THE EXCHANGE OF IGNORANCE.

Do not let anyone steal your peaceful control!

Darwin's Deadly Descendants The Holocaust

Have you ever thought about how much damage and evil Charles Darwin (1809-1882) has created? Think about the trailing results of this lunatic and his descendants. One of them was born in Austria. He helped create the National Socialist German Worker's (Nazi) Party after World War I. Who? Adolph Hitler, born 1889.

Are you aware of the following? This English naturalist, Darwin, published the earth-shattering work called, "On the Origin of Species by Means of Natural Selection or the Preservation of Favored Races in the Struggle for Life," in 1859. This book has had a devastating effect on human existence. So many people have been sucked into this cesspool book and are even teaching it to our children as fact. It is *not* fact!

Adolph Hitler was totally into Darwin's theories – yes, theories. They are not facts, as we have been led to believe. Darwin believed in the 'natural selection' premise, that only the 'fittest' have the right to live. Are you fit? Do you have a right to live? Do you have any type of illness that make you unfit? Diabetes, heart-trouble, high cholesterol or asthma? What is fit? Who determines it? Did Almighty God form you from an amoeba?

Hitler, who vowed to create a superior race, not only killed over six-million Jews, he murdered nearly two-hundred-thousand souls with infirmities. Do you have a crooked leg, arm, shoulder, facial structure, finger or teeth? Do you have a problem seeing (glasses), hearing, or even speaking? Are you tongue-tied? You would have been exterminated. You would have been euthanized, murdered like a worthless animal. He would have declared your eating food a total waste, and until you were 'selected' for experimentation, torture, and eventual murder, you wouldn't be fed. See, evolution declares you an animal!

Many died of starvation while waiting for their 'day' of destruction under this Darwinism theory. I have fibromyalgia and rheumatoid arthritis; I would have been murdered really fast, and probably raped and tortured – perhaps even having my breasts cut off like a beast before my demise. Some victims even had their gold teeth removed before they were murdered – without any anesthesia.

Think about how people standing in their interrogation lines were treated. People would be lined up and forced to stand in line for hours. When they could no longer hold their bladder and wet themselves, they were beaten and humiliated. What about watching your own child be beaten and slaughtered, raped or starved to death? The would hear their children's cries for food or water, but couldn't help them. They couldn't provide anything for their children, not even protection from these Darwinian monsters.

Heads were cut off. Arms, hands, and legs were cut off and the victims were cauterized without anything to help the excruciating pain – just for being a Jew, or a handicapped or defective person. Imagine, there was no anesthesia used for anything the Darwinian beasts did to the people; it wouldn't be wasted on an "animal."

The Third-Reich boasted that it would endure for a thousand years. But instead, it only lasted twelve years and four months, from January 1933 until April 1945. There were over 29 million persons slaughtered just for being handicapped, Jewish, or another form of a lower animal-like being.

It is important that we understand what an awesome and terrible event this was – the uniqueness of their annihilation – so that we can better understand the vast differences between good and evil. We have moral choices. What are yours? Do you believe murdering innocent people is all right? Are you Darwinized? Do you not hate evil?

Hitler wanted to totally remove God from humanity; it's almost done!

Christians have acquiescently ignored evil to allow evil to take over our nation.

The Approximate Chronology of the Holocaust

This holocaust started on January 30, 1933, when German president Paul Von Hindenburg (1847-1934) appointed Adolph Hitler (1889-1945) as Reich Chancellor or Prime Minister.

Hitler co-founded the National Socialist German Worker's (NAZI) Party after World War 1, which raged from 1914 to 1918. It started with socialist ideas just like America is accepting today, and pumping into our children. (Our children are being brain-washed right now in the school system.)

It ended with evil beyond belief.

Within one year, Hitler assumed dictatorial powers. Germany fell completely under the control of the Nazis, and the government launched campaign to exterminate all Jews. By March 23 of 1933, he had established the first concentration camp called *Dachau*. He was moving fast to cleanse out all bad genes and infirmities.

By April 1, 1933 this creep – who idolized Darwin so much for his purpose of cleansing the world of bad and lower-class animals (people) – had proclaimed a boycott of all Jewish-owned businesses. By April 7, 1933, he had booted out all Jews from any civil service and denied anyone access to the bar that was not of 'certified' German beliefs.

This was right after Franklin Delano Roosevelt was inaugurated on March 4, 1933. The new president called a special session of Congress for March 9 1933, and they sat until June 16 – the 'so-called' Hundred Days. Congress rapidly enacted laws drafted by Roosevelt and his "Brain Trust" – a group of LIBERAL advisers. The legislation was known collectively as the "New Deal." I believe he had to have known what deals were spawning on the other side of the world; he was no dummy. However, later he did get involved in the rescue of the victimized people under the Nazis.

Now, we have people in America supporting the Communist Party on our own shores – and in our colleges.

On April 26, 1933, Hitler formed the Gestapo – probably the most vile and violent organization that has ever existed. The Gestapo was to be a 'cleaning machine' to expand the "natural selection" Darwinian propaganda. By May 10, 1933, he burned all of the books by the Jews and any opponents of the German state. This fiend was intent on destroying everything that in any way mentioned their seeds of God – all this while he was only prime minister.

Hey, people, don't you see a parallelism here? Remove God. Rewrite history. Remove freedom and patriotic words from out dictionaries and education systems. Take our protection away by banning all firearms. The people of the Holocaust were disarmed first. They had no way of protecting themselves, or their loved ones, from any evil empire; they were total victims.

Then, on August 2, 1934, President von Hindenburg died. Hitler proclaimed himself Commander-in-Chief. He had become the absolute dictator of the new "Third Reich."

On the very next day, August 3, 1934, the German cabinet joined the new president and pronounced Hitler as Fuehrer. Hitler immediately abolished all freedom of speech. Sound familiar? We are not allowed to pray in public, or read our Bibles, and must watch our speech so that it doesn't 'offend' anyone with hate speech.

As fuehrer, he started the dreadful mass exterminations of all opponents, physically challenged, and Jews. America right now is doing its own mass exterminations with abortion and euthanasia. Abortion is exceedingly painful to the little baby. Think about yourself having your body parts ripped apart; these babies do feel it.

Yes, Darwin followers are ill-equipped and unlearned. They do not care about anyone but themselves. Evolutionists are pagans, and God will judge them.

But whoso shall offend one of these little ones which believe in Me; it were better for him that a millstone were hanged around his neck, and he were drowned in the depth of the sea.
Matthew 18:6

And whosoever shall offend one of these little ones that

believe in Me, it is better for him that a millstone were hanged about his neck, and he were cast in to the sea.

Mark 9:42

It were better for him that a millstone were hanged around his neck, and he cast into the sea, than he should offend one of these little ones.

Luke 17:2

Thou knowest me from the moment of conception. Thine eyes did see My substance, yet being unperfected.

Psalms 139:1-24

There are so many verses in the Bible about God's hands forming us in our mother's womb. And in Psalms 139:16, "HIS eyes did see our substance (what murderers call a blob), yet being unperfect: and in His Book, all our members are written, which were in continuance fashioned, when as yet there were none of them." God is making babies in the womb, and abortionists are destroying something God is working on.

Read Psalms 119:73, Isaiah 44:2, Isaiah 44:24, Job 31:15, and Jeremiah 1:15. These are all talking about God knowing the baby before it came out of the womb...

All abortionists, anyone believing in abortion, need to read this entire chapter of Psalms 139. You cannot be a Christian and believe in murdering babies.

No wonder the evil ones are trying to get the Bible outlawed. The Bible says that *Jesus* knows the babies since conception, and that abortion is murdering a living child. *Jesus* watches them as they grow and are perfected *in the mother' womb!* Then, in 1935, Hitler started putting up many signs in towns, villages, restaurants, and stores, saying, "No Jews." So, it became hard for the Jewish people, handicapped, and 'other' lower-class animals to purchase their daily needs. By September 15, the Reichstag passed the anti-Semitic "Nuremberg Laws."

Can you believe that in 1935, while all this brutality was going on, that Carl von Ossietsky, a German, won the Nobel Peace Prize? There have been many more non-deserving Nobel Peace Prize winners since, just for the appeasement of "the whackos."
In late October, 1936, Hitler and Mussolini formed the Rome-Berlin Axis, a coordinating system to further the National Selection Programs (process). Then on November 25, he signed a military pact with Japan.

When I read this I was amazed, because all the Japanese people I have met are very intelligent. It's curious to me that the Japanese persons in authority would fall for this evil scheme. I had a professor, Yukiko Kimoto, who was probably the smartest woman I have ever met. I loved the gentle strength she had. Professor Yuki didn't talk too much, but everything she said right on! She knew much about everything. I once tried to talk to her about the Japan/American war…and she would only say that there were things happening, and had happened, that the people of both Japan and America knew nothing about. It was a very sad war, and many innocent people on both sides were slaughtered. That was all she would say, and I respected her for not playing a blame game.

July 16, 1937, the Buchenwald concentration camp opened.

Most evolutionists are part of the evil ones – and they are many, both in our schools and in our workplaces! Teaching our children that we "just evolved" from apes. They are trying to remove God from all our schools and books; they want a godless society run by the state or government…just like Hitler did.

False prophets rule with fear: Nehemiah 6:14, First Thessalonians 4:6 and First John 4:1…can you see the parallel of how the 'politicians' are trying to put fear into the people of America right now? These promoters of fear and rebellion are not wanting to rule according to God's Word. God will judge them, and they will lose their ill-gotten gain and power when they stand before the Great White Throne of Almighty God to be judged for all their iniquities against God's people.

Another scary fact is that we have communist teaching in our universities. That certainly isn't doing anything for free speech or truth. What will the next freedom be that will be taken away from us in the dirty slope to a dictator? Will we lose our guns, our protection…or our free speech, it seems to have begun already? Our monies? We already are having our money confiscated to support those that do not want to work. God said, "If a man (or woman) won't work, they don't deserve to eat." Almost everyone can do something!!!

By March 13, 1938, the Third Reich had 'annexed' and taken over Austria. The Nazis applied all of the anti-Semitic laws to the beautiful little country. If you haven't seen *"The Sound of Music"* movie, you should. It tells about part of the Nazi takeover and occupation of this once-gorgeous homeland. It's a true story and really gripping. Make sure you watch the 1965 version (before it was re-invented). It will make you laugh and cry as you see a small portion of how immoral, controlling and devastating the Nazi's were. How the people were sucked into losing their country…

On July 6, 1938, there was an international conference at Evian, France. From that date pm. France refused to provide refuge for German Jews. They were afraid of this evil and twisted Darwin-inspired country called Germany. They were not strong enough to fight them…so they became a subordinate to Hitler.

But the madman's insatiable appetite for power and gene selection perpetuated the Munich Agreement on September 29 of 1938, where Britain and France 'accepted' German annexation of Sudetenland, a part of Czechoslovakia – whereby Hitler speeded up his conquest for power and gene cleansing. By October 5, 1938, all passports of Jews were marked with the letter *J.* November 7, 1938, Herschel Grynszpan, whose parents were deported from Germany to Poland, assassinated Ernst von Rath, Third Secretary of the German Embassy in Paris. I know of nothing more written about him.

March 15, 1939 brought about the total occupation of Czechoslovakia by the Germans. Many Jews lived in the country at the time and were scheduled to be exterminated like animals. On July 26, of 1939, Adolph Eichmann was placed in charge of Prague, a branch of the emigration office. He was evil to the core and relished in abusing the 'animals.'

Then came the Soviet-German Non-Aggression Pact of August 23rd. I guess Hitler figured the Soviet Union was a bit too large to take over at that time. He needed to build up more troops first.

But poor little Poland; on September 1, 1939, the German army invaded this peaceful little country. This was the beginning of World War II, which lasted from 1939-1945.

Finally, on September 3, 1939, Britain and France declared war on Germany. And by the seventeenth, the Soviets took over Eastern Poland in a first step to stopping Germany. After the Soviets took over the Eastern part of Poland, Jews from Moravia and Austria were sent to occupied Poland, where they were finally "safe" – at least safer than they had been.

How could it take so long for other countries to accept what was being done to so many helpless people? Why didn't other countries stand up and say no? I'm sure many of the 'Allied' countries were looking the other way, and perhaps, even had their own presence of 'gene selection.' Darwin-followers kept things that were right from being done.

November 9, 1939 brought the 'Kristallnacht' or "Night of Broken Glass." Anti-Semitic riots raged in Germany and Austria. Synagogues were destroyed, shops looted, and people slaughtered. (Sound familiar? Is this America now under Communism?)

On the twelfth of November, 26,000 Jews were arrested and sent to concentration camps that very same day, and the monsters didn't have to have a reason for the arrests; it was just an order from the state.

November 15, 1939, brought the banishment of all Jewish children from German schools. Jews were animals and learning was a waste of time.

November 23, the wearing of *Judenstern* – a six-pointed Star of David – was made mandatory throughout *occupied Poland* to make an exhibition of and humiliate the Jewish people.

December 1, 1939, a decree on "Aryanization," or a compulsory expropriation of Jewish industries, businesses, and shops were enacted, and the Jewish people were left with nothing to sustain themselves. They were at the total mercy of the Nazis in their efforts to 'gene select' the world.

1940, and the Germans were still on the march. They invaded Denmark and Norway on April 9, 1940. By April 30th, Poland was sealed off, and the ghetto at Lodz was established.

May 10, 1940, saw the Nazis invade Holland, Belgium, and France. June 4th, in fear, the British Army evacuated its forces from Dunkirk, France. By June 22nd, France surrendered to the Germans.

September 15, 1940, wearing of the Jewish Star is decreed throughout the Greater Reich, or all that Germany controlled.

September 23, 1940, brought about the first experiments with gassing the people. This was done at Auschwitz.

September 27, 1940, the Berlin-Rome-Tokyo Axis was established, forcing the alignment of Rome and Tokyo to Germany. November 15, 1940, the Warsaw ghetto was sealed off.

After pledging not to, Germany attacks the Soviet Union on June 22, 1941. You cannot trust the words of liberals, they lie! Hitler was the most ultra-liberal that has ever lived. He was truly a demon. About three weeks later, on July 8th, the wearing of the Jewish Star was decreed in the German-occupied Baltic States, including Finland (Aland), Denmark (Bornholm), and Sweden (Gotland).

July 31, 1941, Reinhard Heydrich (1904-1942) was appointed by Hermann Wilhem Goering (Goring) (1893-1946) to carry out "The Final Solution," the total extermination of all Jews in Europe.

THE HOLOCAUST WAS IN FULL SWING.

October 10, 1941, The Resienstadt ghetto in Czechoslovakia was established for the poor Jewish people who had nowhere to go and no way to support themselves.

On October 14, 1941, the deportation of German Jews began. This was followed by a massacre in Odessa on October 23 with 34,000 dead, and a massacre in Kiev on October 29th, with another 34,000 dead. Yet another massacre in Rovno left 15,000 more dead.

See how one thing can mushroom into a monster when good people turn a blind eye and not challenge evil?

Perhaps Darwin didn't realize the horrific chain of events he was creating; perhaps he did and just didn't care. Most evolutionists don't want truth, just power and the elimination of God.

Where were the "good" people of the world? Why didn't someone help these defenseless people? Britain tried, but was no match for the German Nazis. The world turned a deaf ear and a blind eye to the plight of these precious people. Oh, "they" knew what was going on, but "they" didn't want to get involved in making things right.

THEY WERE COWARDS! If you don't stand up for what is right in our society now, you are a coward! Our children are going to Hell because you won't stand up for truth!

December 7, 1941, the Japanese attacked Pearl Harbor. Now there were two fronts to the war. December 8, the United States enters the war – finally, now that it affects us. On that same day, December 8, the Chelmno Extermination Camp on the Ner River in Poland is opened up, no more 'safe' place for the Jewish refugees. This time it wasn't called a concentration camp; it was called what it was: an extermination camp.

On that same day, December 8, 1941, the Germans massacred 27,000 in Riga. Then on December 22nd, another 32,000 in Vilna were exterminated like animals.

Then came 1942. There was a Wannsee Conference on the Nazis, the "Final Solution of the Jewish Problem," or the bad genes, on January 20, 1942.

On January 21, 1942, the Jewish people decided they were going to die anyway, they might as well go down fighting. They established a unified resistance organization in the Vilna ghetto. The Jewish Resistance groups courageously and dangerously expanded in number throughout Eastern Europe.

June 1, 1942, the Treblinka death camp opened. Wearing of the Jewish Star was decreed in Nazi-occupied France and Holland. **Three hundred thousand** Jews from the Warsaw ghetto were deported to the Treblinka death camp for extermination on July 22nd, men, women – and children. The children were usually taken from the mother; the father had already been separated to the men's station, castrated (at least bulls get anesthesia to become steers), and forced to be slaves until their 'time' was at hand.

Try to imagine the horror those mothers were going through. Not only were their husbands gone, but their children were yanked, screaming, from their arms. The children were made slaves – both labor and sexual – until the little "monkeys" were 'selected.'

By the 28th of July, 1942, the Jewish resistance organization had established itself in the Warsaw ghetto. And June to September, 1942, hundreds of Jewish partisans left the Vilna ghetto for the forest, where they continued their resistance to the Nazis. They had heard that the Allied Nations were on the move. There was finally a glimmer of hope, however faint.

September 23, 1942, all hope vanished again, when there was a liquidation of everyone left at the Vilna ghetto.

October 27, 1942, allied nations finally pledged to punish Germans for their policy of genocide.

January 14 to 24, 1943, President Roosevelt, Winston Churchill and General Charles de Gaulle met in Casablanca, Morocco, where they each pledged to fight until the Germans surrendered unconditionally.

January 18, 1943, the Jews in the Warsaw ghetto launched an uprising against Nazi deportations. Street fighting lasted only four days. These unarmed people were fighting for their lives, with anything they could get their hands on, but they were no match for the well-equipped Nazis.

February 2, 1943, the German Sixth Army surrendered at Stalingrad. This marked the turning point in the war.

Why does it take so long for 'good people' to accept the facts that there is a real and present evil out there, and WE as God's people are to combat evil? **Forty-one times** *in the Bible, GOD sent judgment* **by way of weather** *to people that would not stand up and fight for Israel and the Jews. HE said, "I will bless those that bless you (Israel), and I WILL curse those who do not." We are still to be standing up for God's chosen people. God hasn't changed His mind. Not to do so will bring damnation on you - and even your Country. God said Israel must not be divided...and yet look at it now...even the Arabs were given the West Bank...Now they are even talking of dividing Jerusalem...If they do...watch out people...judgment will fall!!!* **God never changes...**

April 19, 1943, after hearing of the surrender at Stalingrad, the Jews in the Warsaw ghetto began fighting anew. This time the fighting lasted for weeks. Again, they were fighting for their lives, and for the lives of their families. They knew what had happened to their 300,000 predecessors – families and friends. But this time there seemed to be a spark of hope.

Yet, their hope faded quickly because the day of May 16, 1943, brought about the liquidation of the Warsaw ghetto; everyone was exterminated. On June 11, 1943, Heinrich Himmler (1900-1945) ordered liquidation of all Polish-Jewish ghettos to keep down any resistance.

August 2, 1943, there was a revolt at Treblinka's death camp, and one at Bailystok ghetto on August 16th.

October 20, 1943, the United Nations War Crimes Commission was established, before the United Nations itself was fully established.

1944 begins; May 15 to June 8, 476,000 Jews were deported from Hungary to Auschwitz. The Nazis were getting desperate and anxious to complete their "cleansing" of the bad genes in their attempt to mandate the "natural selection" genome.

June 4, 1944, the Allies landed in Rome. June 6 was D-Day, and Allied invasion of Nazi-occupied Western Europe. The invasion was called "Operation Overload." At dawn, the Allies crossed the Channel to Northern France. There were more than 5,000 ships, mostly small landing crafts, carrying almost 100,000 men. There were 1, 083 bombers and some 2,000 fighter planes overhead when they hit the beaches of Normandy.

Can you just imagine the show? It was spectacular! Our beautiful Marines had landed! Praise the Lord, Help was on its way!

History repeats itself, so it is very important to remember what happened here to avoid it happening again to us! We cannot overlook evil, we cannot condone people taking over us or our Country. We must nip it in the bud, before it spreads to the point of no return. Communism has entered our Nation, both on the private and the political levels. We must root them out and replace them with God-fearing men and women.

The Nazis were deeply entrenched in Normandy, and they fought grimly. But within a week, the Allies had conquered the beach-heads for the drive across France. It began in Normandy, France. Remember our gorgeous Marines putting up our United States Flag in Normandy. Never forget that! It spoke freedom – freedom and right!

Beginning on June 13, 1944, Hitler unleashed his promise of "secret weapons," the V-1 and later the V-2 rockets. They did hurt many people, but they were no match for our allied troops. Hitler's last "great" counterattack was from December 16, 1944, to January 16, 1945. This skirmish is known as the "Battle of the Bulge in the Ardennes."

November 24, 1944, Himmler ordered the destruction of the Auschwitz crematoria as the Nazis tried to hide the bodies and evidence of the death camps and torture they had inflicted on these innocent people. They dug huge holes for mass graves, and pushed the bodies of the victims into them with plows. Some were not even dead yet.

January 17, 1945, the Soviet troops entered Eastern Prussia and extended their conquest of Czechoslovakia and Hungary; they liberated Warsaw, and by April were driving toward Berlin.

February 4 – 10, 1945, saw the Yalta Conference in the Crimea; Roosevelt, Churchill, and Stalin agreed Russia would enter the war against Japan.

On March 5, 1945 (some history books say March 7), the American and Allied troops crossed the Rhine River and overran the German troops. April 11, 1945, the American troops liberated the Buchenwald death camp.

On April 12, 1945, President Franklin Delano Roosevelt died of a cerebral hemorrhage in Warm Springs, Georgia. His Vice-President, Harry S. Truman took over the office of Presidency…and then won the election in 1948.

April 15, 1945, British troops liberated the Bergen-Belsen death camp.

April 25, 1945, at a juncture of Soviet and U.S. troops Torgau on the Elbe; the beginning of the demise of Nazi Germany was marked.

April 30, 1945, was a great day; Hitler committed suicide at his capital. This was ten days after his fifty-sixth birthday, on April 20th. His wife (some say they were not actually married, I don't know), Eva Braun, (history reports) also killed their children, but they never had any children. The children in the bunker with them belonged to Magda and Joseph Goebbels. According to the most reliable accounts, Magda gave her children morphine shots and cyanide pills before killing herself.

The German troops were a mess and fragmented. So, on May 7, 1945, the successor German regime surrendered unconditionally at Rheims, France, spelling the end of the war in Europe. Dwight

David Eisenhower was Supreme Commander of the troops at that time.

June 23, 1945, the Soviet summer offense began, and Soviet troops liberated the Maidanek death camp.

October 23, 1945, Allied armies liberated Paris. They should remember this…They were liberated, yet they didn't want to 'get involved' in the liberating of someone else.

August 15, 1945, Japan surrendered unconditionally. This was the end of World War II.

And on November 22, 1945, the Nuremberg War Crimes Tribunal commenced. The Nuremberg trials lasted until October 1, 1946, which happened to the Day of Atonement, or Yom Kippur.

There was a judgment in which twelve defendants were sentenced to death, three to life imprisonment, four to various terms, and three were acquitted.

War is ugly. Many innocent people die. This could happen in America with all the apathy that has sprung up in our Christian community. Preachers behind pulpit are no longer preaching out of the Bible…but pulling their sermons off the 'Web', written, mostly, by people who really do not know what the Word of God say.

Sermons are to come from God's Word…

Where are the sermons warning about Hell? I've been visited several churches in my travels in the last few years. Not once did I hear a pastor warn his/her flocks about the fact that there is a real Hell, and sin, both open and hidden, will put them there. Christianity is full of 'feel good' preachers and teachers now. The blood of their flocks and students will be on their hands…and on YOURS when you don't tell people the truths of the Bible…

Discrimination

Talk about something stupid; people discrimination in any form is stupid! If you are a people-discriminating person, you are stupid! Think about this: if every flower was the same color – how much of the beauty of our world would be gone?

What color would everything be? Can you imagine everything black – black trees, no green leaves, not any vibrant and colorful flowering blooms on them. No richly colored fruit? You would have black grapes, black strawberries, black oranges…would they still call them oranges – since there wouldn't be any color called orange? If you picked a grape, you wouldn't know what it was, a grape or a Bing cherry. How about a black ball; is it an orange, a grapefruit, a lemon – or a pomegranate? There would be no beautiful red apples, nor golden yellow ones.

Imagine the entire world without any beautiful, luscious, green grass. Many people have colored rock in their front or rear yards for landscaping. But what if all rock were black? You would have black sidewalks, black houses, black cars…and a black sky – how dreary.

We would never know there are billowy white clouds in the blue sky, that we often see artwork in as we search for images. I wouldn't be able to let my active imagination run wild with picking things out of the cloud formations; like a face, or an animal, or an island. (That's a really good game for traveling with kids, big and small.) There would be no fun looking at black clouds in a black sky…

If all spiders were all black, you wouldn't be able to tell them apart. You wouldn't know if one had a violin or an hour-glass on it. You couldn't know which ones were poisonous and which were not. I like to watch a little spider spin its web. It's interesting how they seem to tie a knot at each juncture to keep the strand in place. How do they do that? God told them to.

What about snakes? You wouldn't be able to see the "diamonds" on a rattlesnake, nor the pretty gopher snake that eats bad things around your home and yard. You would probably kill all snakes, even the good ones, with your black stick. I had the prettiest little gopher snake in my back yard for a short period. He got used to me coming out and lifting up 'his' little rock to see if he was there, and didn't even slither away. His little tongue was moving in and out as though he was really listening to me. I was sorry when he disappeared. If everything had been black, I wouldn't have gotten to enjoy the little guy for a spell.

I know Satan is always portrayed as a snake, but it's a different kind of snake than these little creatures that are good for our environments. Satan is not good for our environment…or anything else? I don't like rattlers, but even they are pretty.

Take the skunk, it is a beautiful creature. But, if it were all black you wouldn't know to give it the right-of-way…

Let your mind wander, really wander. A black world would have no light or beauty. Our awesome God knew we would enjoy colors, so he created them for our enjoyment. It is so disgusting for someone to disunite people because of their different colors of melatonin in their skins. That's the only difference in the races…

their skin color. They all think, feel, love, hate, get hungry and have to go potty. All the same way.

God created light so we could see all of his beautiful colors. Living in an all-black world would be very depressing. God knows that. Yellow is a happy color, and when you have yellow around you, it helps you feel better. But what if everything was all yellow, or all white or even all red?

The Creator of the Universe knew if everyone He created was one color, we would be robbed of so much joy. Yes, I said joy. Knowing people of different colors, all God's creations, is exciting. I have friends from all colors, and each brings a special measure of pleasure to what could be a doldrums existence.

One good friend of mine, who happens to be black, is so good for my spirit. We laugh together about the fact that when God put the extra pigment in her skin, He also put extra rhythm in her rump. She cannot stand or sit still if there is music anywhere around; something on her will be moving. She really helped me appreciate different kinds of music.

What if we only had one NOTE in music? It would be dull… dum…dum…dum… I am so happy that we have all the different notes we do. One note cannot make melody, many different ones do.

I love going to a 'black' church. We've been out to our local Air Force Base with a longtime serviceman friend, Ken. Ken is so blonde that he almost glows. We stick out like sore thumbs, so I know what a black, brown, yellow or red person feels like sometimes going to a 'white' church. If you don't make them feel welcome when they walk into your church, you are not filled with the love of *Jesus* Christ!

I must admit, one of the thing I enjoy the most about the 'black' church is that during the musical worship time, even the babies are keeping time with the music. The church sways and stomps and rejoices in the Lord. I've always thought, especially after my first visit to a 'black' church, that God was no doubt enjoying his little ones that he added extra rhythm to worship Him. These gorgeous Spirit filled children really get involved in praise, and it's like a bit of the real Heaven right here on earth. And the preaching- WOW! The sanctuary rings with amens and hallelujahs. If you, as a white person, or any other color, want a blessing, visit a black church.
A good friend of mine sent me his own true story:

His roommate from college was black. He visited his friends home church one weekend after they had gone to a concert. He said (his friend), "I was just about to get you up."

"What time does church start?" My friend asked.
"Ten." Replied my friends' roommate.

"Ummmm…Aren't we late?" My friend asked.

"Ohhh!" he said, "don't worry. We'll get there about 11, and they'll still

Be singing. I made pancakes. Eat good. We'll be there awhile."

Sure enough, it was 2:30 before we got out of there, and I was never bored for even a second.

My husband and I once too my mother to a 'white' church. She was getting elderly and couldn't hear very well. She had started talking loudly as if the other people were hard of hearing too. As soon as the service was finished, and we were on the way out of the sanctuary, she said very loudly, "I don't think I want to come back to this church again; it's dead!"

My husband and I were so embarrassed because everyone heard her. We ushered her out to the car as fast as we could…without meeting anyone's eyes.

But she was right. We did not feel the presence of the Lord in the service, or in the people. We didn't want to go back either.

I have also had the pleasure of going to a Hispanic church. "Wow" is the only way you can explain a Mexican church. Beautiful music rang clear from the rafters, and tears of joy streaked the cheeks of both men and women. I looked at most of the ladies' hair, full and beautiful. Mine is so thin that I have to backcomb it to cover the thinning spots. I sometimes wonder if the Mexicans have a special 'hair' gene because of all their beautiful heads of hair.

Their church was filled with joy, and there is no way anyone could have stayed in a depressed mood. Plus, they usually have goodies after the service, and can most of those ladies cook, even the young ones. I love Mexican food and sometimes I hope I haven't made too much of a pig of myself…

Acts 16:31 says, "Believe on the Lord *Jesus* Christ and thou shalt be saved." It doesn't say – "If you are Lutheran, or Baptist, or Assembly of God, or Church of God. It only says, "IF you believe, (even if you're Catholic) that *Jesus* Christ is who He said He is; that He died on an old rugged cross, shed His blood for our sins and salvation; that He was buried in a tomb and raised the third day from the grave; and that He is now in Heaven sitting on the right hand of His Father, Almighty God. We must believe that His blood can wash all of our sins away – yes, even the Methodists – and that when we die, if we have accepted Him as our Savior and Lord, and commit to live His commandments to the best of our ability, we will go to Heaven and live in a mansion He is preparing for us. Yes, even for the Presbyterians. Your denomination is not the important thing.

Your 'denomination' is just a religion. Your only way to Heaven is through the blood of The Lord *Jesus* Christ. There is no other way!!!

When Almighty God rolled that huge stone away from the sepulcher – He rolled it right over Satan's back…Slewfoot is now working with a broken back. So, *IN THE MIGHTY NAME OF JESUS, YOU* have authority over the evil one. Not in your own power but in the Name that is above all other names *Jesus* Christ.

Our omnipotent God created different color of people, just as He did different colors of flowers and fruit. We are all God's flowers, and He purposely made us different, He didn't want us all alike. Our Lord enjoys our differences, and so should we. Heaven will be a virtual kaleidoscope of colors, to the degree that our minds cannot comprehend the overwhelming beauty. If we would just quit our foolishness of the evil of discrimination, we could enjoy more of Gods kaleidoscope he has given us right here on earth.

Get off your discrimination damnation train. Get over it!

A really good black friend of mine is a riot. We not only poke fun at each other about our colors, but with Jan being a bit plump, as am I, we get silly laughing together about our 'plumpness.' She has perfect beautiful white teeth, and I have a flipper; not quite a bridge, but it covers the two teeth on my right side that are missing…and does she have a blast with that. Talking about my black hole… When I smile with my flipper in, I don't have a black hole.

We both have the same kind of blood, all people have essentially the same, it just has various negative/positive differences. But it's all red. If she cuts herself, her blood is a beautiful rich, dark, healthy red. But when I cut myself, or get a pinprick… mine is much lighter because of an iron deficiency.

Jan's a marvelous cook – I can burn water in the microwave.

She's a fantastic housekeeper, in fact she takes new washcloths and makes footsies out of them for people to put on when they take their shoes off before entering her home. And we get to keep them.

She is my sister in the Lord, I would be proud to have her as my blood sister. She loves the Lord with all her heart. When I'm feeling down, she knows it and perks me up with her wonderful words of wisdom, and even her sense of humor about the races. She's a real crackerjack! Laughing at yourself is good medicine.

If you have all black friends, you are narrow-minded. If you have all white friends, you are an idiot. If you have all brown friends, you are a loser. You are missing so much.

If you get offended if someone refers to you as Black, White, Hispanic, Chinese, Japanese or Jewish…get over it. God made you that way. That's the way God made you. You are colored for God's enjoyment. Almighty God wanted each one of us to look like we do for HIS pleasure. Revelation 4:11, "For thy pleasure they are and we are created."

Ooops! It sounds like we were all created equal…no greater and no lesser, so get over your racism and discrimination, you were not created for yourself…you were created for Almighty God.

Multicolor is magnificent. I believe we will still be the same color in Heaven forever. So, we had better learn to live with each other now, or we might not make it to God's unimaginable kaleidoscope!

Jesus is Jewish!

Dishwashers Our Maids?

It's time for a bit of lightheartedness – as well as practical tips. Almost everyone who knows me laughs at me because of my love of my dishwasher (my maid). That's right, my dishwasher. Our friends even tease my husband, asking him if I try to put him in the dishwasher also…or our twenty-five-pound cat Big Kitty (who we lost a few years ago).

If you are in the market for a new dishwasher, here are a few tips to make your dishwasher your friend also.

First and foremost, get a good one. Mine is six-year-old and still works well under the heavy demand I push at it. Mine is a heavy-duty Kenmore.

Secondly, don't buy one with a center arm; they get in the way. Buy one with an arm clear up in the top, and one at the very bottom. You must have two arms. Don't let a salesperson tell you that one arm works all right; it doesn't!

Third, get one that has the one side geared to larger objects, such the turntable out of your microwave or a large baking sheet.

Fourth, get one that the top rack comes out for washing large things, really important.

I usually always add a one-half cup of bleach to the bottom just before I start it. I find this helps to keep stains out of cups and glasses; besides, it disinfects the inside of your dishwasher at the same time. It helps keep the musty smell down too. As you read along, you will see why I have to disinfect the inside each time I run it.

I do not use the heat cycle, only air. Heat costs too much for electricity and will ruin many things put inside. I also try to use most of the electric I use before 9:00 a.m. or after 9:00 p.m. Most companies, ours included, have lower rates between those hours. When you use one as much as I do…it saves significantly on the electric bill.

I let the dishwasher do a lot of my cleaning for me. My mother instilled in me the desire to have a clean home. (Hear that ladies? YOU teach your children to be clean.) I am very busy most of the time, as I know you are too, so any helping "hands" are welcome. There were six of us stair-step kids at home, and to this day, I don't know how she kept the house clean…or her sanity. Especially when she didn't have any 'modern conveniences.'

So here are some of the things I let my "maid" do:

1. Animal dishes (not the animals.)
2. Bathtub stools
3. Belts
4. Brushes from cooking
5. Car mats (this works great)
6. Chairs (I've even taken apart a few chairs and ran the seats, backs, arm pads, as well as the legs and casters through. Casters get so gunked up icky.)
7. Cleaning pails

8.   Cleaning sponges (In fact, every time I do a load of dishes, I run my sink sponges through; it can become the dirtiest item in your kitchen, next to your can opener.)
9.   Combs
10.   Dishpans
11.   Draining racks and boards
12.   Electric cords (BUT be sure you wait twenty-four hours before using them. You may not want to try this. I hate cruddy-looking electric cords.)

I'll put a disclaimer right here. Neither my publisher nor I are responsible for you putting anything in the dishwasher just because I do. Think for yourself, I can't! What works for me may not work for you.

---

13.   Electric and gas range top elements. (Be sure and allow to dry thoroughly before plugging back in.)
14.   Filters and dispensers from the clothes washer and dryer.
15.   Fingernail and toenail clippers. (These really harbor germs.)
16.   Garden hoses (Usually have to be done alone, quite heavy.)
17.   Grab bars
18.   Grandkid's booster seats and car seats
19.   Grandkid's little padded cartoon toilet seat (This fits on the top of the big seat.)
20.   Hairbrushes (Remove as much hair as possible first.)
21.   In-Out baskets on my desk

22. Lawn furniture cushions (The smaller ones that will fit.)
23. Light globes
24. Needlepoint and plastic tissue covers
25. Plastic three-ring binders
26. Plastic storage boxes and shelves

27. Pump dispensers for soap, shampoo, or hand lotion. (They all get really dirty during use, and this cleans out underneath the rims and makes the pump look new.)
28. Purses
29. Refrigerator and stove racks and drawers
30. Rubber mats (Including tub and shower mats.)
31. Scissors (Especially cooking ones.)
32. Scotch tape dispenser
33. Sink mats
34. Small PVC tables (On some models the legs even come apart for complete   cleaning.)
35. Small step stools
36. Soap dishes
37. Some lamp shades (But, be careful which ones.)
38. Stove burner covers (They really get gross, but be sure you get the heavy baked   enamel, or porcelain ones; the cheap ones will peel.)
39. Thermos containers (Have side seam on bottom and upside down to drain well   when you remove.)
40. Tools (Dry very well; then WD-40 each – but no electric tools.)
41. Toothbrushes (They get really germy and need to be sterilized at least once a week,   or replaced.)
42. Toys

43.   Various racks

44.   Vent over cooking range (It usually snaps in and out and gets really grimy.)

45.   Wastebaskets – these are a biggie… (I keep aplastic bag in mine, like the ones I get at the grocery store. Then when I take the garbage and papers out, I take most of the germs too. Just put a clean bag I to replace the one you take out. About once a month, I take out the top rack and put small wastebaskets in and run through the dishwasher. It's scary and dangerous how many germ and bugs hide in wastebaskets and garbage pails; you need to keep them clean, especially if you have an allergenic family…like me. Dirty waste baskets will also draw ants.)

46.   Whatnots (Be selective and careful, however.) There are many more items I could list, but I think you get the idea. I let my dishwasher work for me. I like having a maid. But remember, you run any of this list at your own risk. Also, don't mix a lot of stuff with your dishes. Toothbrushes are alright. I do not wash my dishes before I put them in the dishwasher, but I do rinse the loose food off of them.

I love the fact that my maids top rack comes out and I can wash tall things in her. That saves me a lot of time on oven racks, etc.…

Since I like my kitchen counters clean, I also use my dishwasher for storing dirty dishes until it gets full enough to run. I don't usually run a partial load, which wastes water and electricity. However, when you are storing dirty dishes, be sure and shut the door completely to avoid bugs, like ants, from taking up residence… because they will.

I don't like a sink filled with dirty dishes; it is so outlandish, lacking in polish and grace. I also shudder at a counter that is full of junk and leftover crumbs. That's where our food is prepared; it should be kept clean. Even young children can be taught to bring their dishes to the sink so you can put them in the maid.

Children need to be taught from an early age that your home is not a luxury hotel, and that *everyone* must have duties to keep it running efficiently. To not teach your children is not being a good parent with preparing them to take care of themselves.

NOTE; Anytime you have any kind of meat touch anything – including your sink, counter, chopping board, or utensils…sterilize them. Serious germs grow out of old blood or secretions from meats. I love the Clorox disinfecting wipes. They are great for a quick cleanup and germ elimination. I always wipe my counters and inside the microwave with them. The turntable of my microwave, and the rollers, of course, go in the dishwasher. But more often, if a spill occurs, I wipe down the inside walls and door with disinfecting wipes. It is so fast and easy.

To me, a dirty kitchen is reflective of a possible ding-dong dweller. And I wouldn't want to eat at their house.

Don't be a DDD. Keep that kitchen clean!!!
☺ ☺ ☺

Always remember, you use things, not people!

Update: I saw a news cast on Fox News. It was on how dirty and germy all sponges become almost immediately! It made me irky. I threw away all my kitchen sponges. I only use a paper towel like a sponge, then toss it. Not all paper towels will stand being used like a sponge, but I use Bounty, and it seems to work the best.

When I saw all the microscopic germs moving around on this 'clean' sponge, I really got sick to my stomach.

I am also using paper towels now to dry my dishes, then toss them too.

Think about it…

ELOISE – MY TERROR-FLEEING FRIEND

It really did happen!

There has been a movement for some time to not only rewrite history, but to destroy a bunch of it. To believe some of those morally deranged, perverted, so-called historians, the Holocaust never took place. I'm here to tell you it did!

THIS IS A TRUE STORY!

I had a friend in my teen years: Eloise. I always knew the last name I knew her by was not her real name. Her parents had been at the Auschwitz crematoria, where they had their tongues cut out so they couldn't talk, and were beaten mercilessly, and tortured continuously.

Eloise and I were friends for over two years before I was even allowed at her home. Her parents were very nice people, but obviously still terribly traumatized. They never went out of their home.

My friend did all the shopping by foot; she didn't have a car – or even a bicycle. They were still so terrified they didn't want anyone to be able to trace them – for fear of more treachery, and no one would stand up for them again; they would be deported back to Germany.

It was when I started walking with Eloise to the store, so she didn't have to carry groceries all alone, that her folks finally let me come into their home, so I could set the groceries on the table instead of the front stoop. At first, I had to leave them at the curb, where my friend would carry them from the curb back to the garage they were living in by herself. It was just a path that was often-times muddy, and many times her shoes showed off the mud-cakes from the rain.

The lady that owned the garage they were hiding in, also owned a small drug store at the front of the lot, with a small apartment above if for her residence. I saw her, more than once, take a big pot of stew back to the folks. This lady was a true Servant of God. I never found out how she had become connected with Eloise's family.

Their little garage home, at the back of a deep lot, was where they lived their meager existence. They had almost no furniture in the one room home, that sported a dirt floor. There was a very used electric hot plate with two burners for cooking. A small table sat in the middle, with 3 mismatched wooden chairs, that looked very dangerous to sit on. A small black cast iron heating stove sat at one end, with wood stacked around it, and a pipe extending through the wall for a vent. There were two rings on top of it, with indentations for a 'lifter' so it could be used for a cook stove when heated. Three 'army like' cots for beds lined up on the back wall. Old fashioned wooden orange crates were stacked up for kitchen cabinets not too far from the table. And another stack by the beds for clothes, etc...

I remember meeting them for the first time. Eloise had

told me they had their tongues cut out by the Germans, and talked funny… Being the airhead sixteen-year old, that fact didn't stick in my mind - until I met them.

It was very hard to act normal (whatever that is) upon meeting them. They were very small. He was probably almost five-feet tall, and she wasn't more than four-and-a-half feet tall. I knew Eloise was small, but was still unprepared to meet this precious couple. Their skin was wrinkled like much older people, and they had no teeth (part of the German torture). He was almost completely bald, only a few hairs sticking up on the top of his head. She had super thin stringy shoulder length hair, with her scalp visible almost in its entirety.

When Eloise introduced me to them, they both tried to greet me, although they neither took my extended hand to shake. When I watched for her father's right hand to extend to me, I saw why he didn't want to shake; his wrist had been broken, in the concentration camp I assumed, so he could never write again…and it was bent crooked and drawn up like a birds' foot. I was completely 'blown away' at the noise they were making as they tried to communicate their greeting. I will NEVER forget those verbal groans. Even after all these years, I can still hear the noise in my minds-eye. I wanted to vomit, but managed to 'hold it' until I was safely away from their home. To add to this, her mother kept trying to cough, and each time she would gag.

Eloise worked full time to support her parents, while going to school full time. She was my special friend. My heart ached when she talked. A lot of my stories about the true Holocaust come from her. She was such a brave young woman.

Then I made a horrible mistake. I was only seventeen, and seventeen-year-olds sometimes don't think beyond their noses regarding consequences. I didn't even give what the ramifications might be a thought. I befriended a young German boy, and acquired a teenage crush on him. I told Eloise about him, and she recognized his name as being very German; I didn't know…I never asked people what race they were before I accepted them as a friend.

She immediately cut off our precious bonds as she took off, without a word. Eloise was not in school the next day, so I went to her home after school to check on her.

Eloise and her family had moved out in the middle of the night, lock, stock and barrel. I had no idea of where they could have vanished to.

Oh, people, be careful who you befriend or hang around with; be so careful as to what feelings your friends, tried and true, are experiencing. This young man was certainly not a Nazi, but his name was obviously German, and I should have put two and two together, and not subjected my terrorized friend to another disaster. In that moment, she became struck with the terror that I, in a weak or dumb moment, might say something that would lead to her parents being found.

A few years later, the nice lady at the drug store told me her parents had died, within just a few weeks of each other, probably from broken hearts. Evidently this Saint had helped them move. I didn't then, nor do I yet, know where they fled to.

Even today, so very many years later, I think about my friend, I see her parents, I can still feel their horror. I can never forget the noises they made trying to speak. I have often grieved for the loss of the bond she and I had shared. The young German boy is long gone. I just didn't think!

I remember how true Proverbs 18:21 is. "The power of life and death are in the tongue."

Charles Robert Darwin lived from 1809 to 1882. He didn't believe in God, which is why he was determined to perpetuate the "Origin of the Species" on us. He wanted to eliminate God. Today, the ultimate goal of the evolutionists is to eliminate God. The evolution teachings are still in the framework of eliminating God. Think about it. You cannot even mention the Lord *Jesus* Christ in prayer without being ostracized.

Do you realize what is going on? Do you have your head in the sand? Can you not comprehend what is going on around you? What happened to all the good people's guts? Why are the good people intimidated so much? Are we on the fast track to gene cleansing again? Are parents to clueless that they are letting their children be indoctrinated into socialism, the precursor to Communism and Nazism? Wake up!!!

We have a powerful and popular lobby called the "Congressional Progressive Caucus," which openly espouses the principals of the Democratic Socialists of America. Do you know what you are voting for? No matter what color someone's skin is, if they are a Socialist and you vote for them, you are anti-American!

Some believe there is such a thing a microevolution, the gradual changing within their own species, but only mentally deficient people believe we came from monkeys. There is no macroevolution! Monkeys do not even have a similar DNA. They have a lesser-number of cells in their DNA.

<u>DNA would not be changed during evolution!</u>

THINK, people, before it's really too late and we become another communist country or succumb to another Nazi Holocaust because we have 'a bad gene' and need to be exterminated. That's where we are headed! Our beloved United States of America is already greatly controlled by Socialists. We already have many communist and Nazi teachers and professors in our schools and universities. Don't be so naïve; a Holocaust IS possible again – right here in America – with evolution's selection of the fittest and with communism and Nazism coming like a runaway freight train.

Stand up for Jesus; He is your salvation and your only hope!

Don't let Satan and his demons have your kids. Teach them absolutes of - and from - the Bible.

Fathers...
Who Needs Them???

In the beginning was the Word and the Word was with God, and the Word was God. I believe that! Do you?

God was in the beginning, and He gave the utterances in the Bible by way of faithful men and women writing under the anointing and direction of His Holy Spirit. Can we not assume that everything in it is correct? The Bible, the whole Bible, is the infallible Word of God, without error. I believe it!

I've heard people say there are errors in the Bible. No, there are no error in the original Manuscript of the Bible. The scribes who translated it only made errors in their translations…The Greek Text has small jot and tittles that just slanting one wrong, can change the meaning. The original manuscript is the inerrant Word of God. God warns us several times not to mess around with his Word or commandments. Read Deuteronomy 4:2 and 12:32, and Revelation 22:18 & 19. It's pretty clear, and a stern warning not to mess around with His Word.

God shall take away his part from the tree of life and from the holy city. *If you mess around and not take the whole Bible as absolute truth, you are on dangerous ground! He, God Himself, will send plagues on you.* I do not read anywhere in the Bible that God has changed His mind. If fact, Malachi 3:6 plainly says, "I AM the Lord, I change not." God never changes.

Having said that, we must bear in mind that Children are a gift to us for a while. They still belong to God. He lets us enjoy them for a season. Be careful what you do to God's property. God tells us in Psalms 127:3,"Behold, children are a gift of the Lord." A gift of love; a piece of God's love, given to us to fill our natural need to love and care for something or someone; a part of God, given to us for a short time…such a short time. If it sounds like I am repeating myself, I am. I want you to remember what I said. The children belong to God! Dare anyone harm God's property?

It seems like only five or six year ago I started my daughter in kindergarten. Now she's gone. She has her own husband, a son and a daughter, a home and job, and her own life. Did I 'train' her up, right? Did I teach her the ways of the Lord? When she is old, will she still be with the Lord?

What an awesome responsibility – a child on loan from God!

How do you get to be father? You must have a child to raise. God most often creates a child from your loins. But very often, God gives you a child because it need's you. It could be an orphan, the result of a family breakup, or an immigrant. In either event, you become a father, ordained of God and accountable to God for your care and actions with that child. God takes fathering very seriously. So should you.

God's order of succession is God first, your spouse second, your child third. These are before your job, friends, cars, computers, televisions, horses, any other family member, or yourself. To be a godly father, you must have the child in its proper place, right next to your spouse, and close to your heart. It is sin to get your life's chain of command out of order. This means that even your mom comes after your wife and children. It's especially notable that a man who puts his job before his wife causes her to cool off toward him and lose respect for him.

Back in Genesis 33:13 and 14, Jacob was pleading with Esau for his children. He said to Esau, "My lord (people of one family often called the man of another family ""my lord""), knoweth the children are frail, and if they are driven hard they will die." He didn't poopoo his children's frailty; he stuck up for it. You are to be sticking up for your children's frailty, also your spouse's.

Jacob said he knew that the children were tender; your children are tender, and you must treat them tenderly. Jacob said that he would lead his family on softly so the children would be able to endure the journey. Do you buffer the endurance of your children? What about your wife's?

Unless you are ready to buffer both your spouse and children over yourself, you should not get married.

How about crying? Do you ever cry? Do you know it's okay to cry? Genesis 37:35 says Joseph's father, Israel, was so beset with grief and crying when he lost Joseph that even his own sons and daughters could not comfort him.

John 11:35 says, *"Jesus* wept." That is the shortest verse in the Bible, but one of the most profound. It showed how much *Jesus* Christ loved Lazarus, and that crying and love go very well together. Never teach your children not to cry; it's okay. *Jesus* was the man of all times, and He wept. Don't tell your sons it's not manly. That's a slap in the face to Christ *Jesus*. We have the responsibility to teach our children to love and to cry, that feelings are okay. (Not always right, but they are okay).

    We also have the responsibility of teaching our children the consequences of both obeying and disobeying. Deuteronomy 11:19 instructs us, "And you shall teach my Commandments to your sons, talking of them when you lie down and when you rise up, when you sit in your house and when you walk along the road." These are commandments, not suggestions. In other words, we are to make time to teach our children the commandments of God in all places. When was the last time you took your child somewhere, one on one, and talked about God, especially His commandments to "love the Lord thy God with all thine heart, with all thine soul and with all thy might?"

    Deuteronomy 6:5, is not one of the original ten, but it follows them with the instructions that these are commandments, the statues, and the judgments, which God commanded, that you are to serve the Lord thy God with all your soul. Have you explained to your child or children that they have a choice, just as the people of Israel had a choice? If they obeyed they would begiven the blessings of rain and food. But if they disobeyed, no rain and no harvests. It was their choice.

    Sin stops our blessings. It's our choice. Do we want God's blessings? Obey and experience the blessings of God, or disobey and suffer the curse of God. Teach your children this that you might snatch their soul from Hell before the 'world' teaches them wrongly. God does curse the world for wrongdoing. In fact, 41 times in the Bible he brought bad weather as judgments for sin.

    Don't give me that garbage about, "We shouldn't influence our children in the choices they make, especially in the matter of religion." **POPPYCOCK.** How is it alright to train our animals, our flowers, our gardens, our hair…but not our children? If we don't train up our children – as the Bible says to do – vulgar advertising will. The newspaper propaganda will. The liquor industry will. The television shows will. The neighbors or peers will. The politicians sure will. The schools with their liberal and ungodly curricula will. Do you really think you should ignore your child's education and choices while they are exposed to all the bastions of Hell? Don't you care enough for them to teach them right and wrong? Unless we train up our children, we are giving them a one-way ticket to the lake of fire. A very real place.

Our sins usually don't affect only us. They hurt others too. God is going to execute vengeance for the breaking of His covenants.

Leviticus 26:32 tells us that God is going to avenge our sins, and it will include our families. Do you really want your family to suffer because of your sin? You are head of the household – God gave you that designation – you are responsible for your family – to God!

God asked for th people to be gathered together to hear His words so they would learn to fear Him all the days they lived on earth and that they were to teach their children the fear of the Lord. Yes, God is loving, but he is also a righteous judge.

Proverbs 1:29 tells us that the fear of the Lord is the beginning of wisdom and knowledge, and that fools despise wisdom and instruction. Seek after knowledge and wisdom; teach your children to seek wisdom and knowledge, lest they be anybody's fool. This is not a shaking, trembling fear, but a healthy and respectful fear. I fear Him; I recognize His power and His omnipotence.

We know, per John 9:31, that God does not hear sinners. But that if anyone is God-fearing and does God's will, then He hears them. Is God hearing you? Are you training up your children in the fear of the Lord so God will hear their cries and prayers?

Proverbs 14:26 tells us, "In the fear of the Lord there is a strong confidence: and His children shall have a place of refuge." Are your children getting confidence from you, knowing you are grounded in the Lord and obey Him?

"Our children" extends right down to our grandchildren, and their children. It even extends to the fatherless children whom God brings into our lives. Proverbs 17:6 says that grandchildren are the crown of old men. I think the Lord is telling us that grandchildren need grandpas to guide them and give them a stability known only to grandparents, and by doing so, Grandpa will be blessed himself

Our grandchildren are a very important part of us, and we shouldn't neglect their welfare or their instruction. Besides, there are at least two places that talk about this in the Bible. One is Proverbs 13:22, it says, "A good man leaveth an inheritance to his children's children." Inheritance includes wisdom. Perhaps this is imparting to us that family ties bind down through the generations, and we never stop being responsible for each other.

The Bible also has much to say about the correcting of a child. God advocates corporal punishment, but NOT CHILD ABUSE. There is a big difference. I managed a medical clinic for several years and had to be in on several child abuse cases. They are tragic and don't train the child, just release anger in the parents. Children suffer so much at the hands of angry, childish, out of control, stupid and screaming parents. Yes, screaming at your child is child abuse. Anger is such selfishness. *NEVER correct a child when you are angry.* Most child abuse starts there. And it only benefits the abuser. Wait until you cool down, think, and then the child can learn the difference between right and wrong, with gentle correction and reasoning. I don't think a child who can be reasoned with needs to have corporal punishment. There are other ways to teach him or her to accept responsibility for their actions. Corporal punishment should be a last resort to small children only. Violence breeds violence, and when you are violent (for your own satisfaction) with your child in their correction, you are not teaching them right, Only wrongly that violence is the answer.

Proverbs 22:15 says, "Foolishness is bound up in the heart of a child; but the rod of discipline will remove it far from him." Here the Bible is referring to an _emblem of authority_ – not a steel rod! If you think it is alright to beat your children with a steel rod, you are an idiot and very unintelligent. Violent punishment is for the parent's satisfaction not for the child's reproof or instruction. It is a totally selfish act. Better watch what you do to these little ones; he or she belongs to God, and you are hurting God's property. **Dangerous, man. Dangerous!**

Proverbs 23:24 states, "The father of the righteous child shall greatly rejoice; and he that begetteth a wise child shall have joy of him." We can be proud of a child who minds. How do you like to be around a child whose parents don't correct him and he is constantly misbehaving? Throwing tantrums, controlling his/her parents (that's what tantrums are: control factors), kicking, screaming, interrupting, throwing things, and the like? Not very pleasant, is it? It's very rude to others – and it shows your lack of wisdom and knowledge. The child should not be allowed to take control of the parent, making the parent the submissive child. If you take control of your child when he/she is small, you usually won't have the problems when they get older.

Child reproof give wisdom, so we are told in Proverbs 29:15,"A child left to himself brings shame." Our prisons and reform schools are full of children left to themselves, children, for the most part, who were never taught right or wrong, never taught respect for other people or their belongings. Never taught to care about other people's feelings; never taught respect for themselves; nor how to accept responsibility for their actions. Many – probably most of the prisoners now in cells around the world -have never had the loving correction of a caring father. Most of these prisoners have never had anyone love them enough to care what happened to them. It's very sad. The 'world' doesn't seem to care what happens to their children anymore. They are too busy with what they want.

If you love your children, you will correct them (not beat them). Many of the prisoners have been victims of child abuse in many forms. They have learned violence at home. They don't know how to be anything but violent. Don't abuse God's children. That is a heinous crime in God's eyes, and judgment WILL fall hard on you. You will be an unfaithful servant, as Matthew 24:51 says, and will actually be cut asunder. This means cut into pieces to live forever where there will be weeping and gnashing of teeth. Imagine the pain! It is dangerous thing to fall into the hands of an angry God…

Do you know that almost always in the Bible, when correction is spoken of, it is the father's duty? You cannot leave the discipline of your children to anyone else.. The Bible says you are the responsible person for their correction and training. The fathers are the ones ultimately responsible for the children's teaching – to God.

Women are mentioned a few times in God's Word as teachers, but very few, and mostly stating that they are to train up, or teach, the younger women how to care for their husbands, children and homes. The actual correcting and punishment is relegated to the fathers. Proverbs 29:17 says, "Correct thy son and he shall give thee rest, comfort, and delight in your soul." Proverbs 22:6 is a famous verse, but do we really hear what it is saying to us? "Train up a child in the way he (or she) should go, and when he/she is old, he will not depart from it." This training must be in the way he should go…according to his ways. The child's habits and interests must be taken into account. What is your child good at? What does he show interest in? It is wrong to try to mold a child into something you want him/her to be and not take into account, and train him, in his individuality and inclinations. Only cattle and sheep are treated alike. Do not treat all you children the same; they have different needs and talents. Cattle and sheep don't excel at anything because there is nothing for them to aim for; they are all alike.

Do you know there are at least five places in Proverbs that Holy Spirit counsels the wise and necessary discipline of children? If you love your children, you will correct them.

Yes, each child is different, wonderful, and a unique little person God created as one of his kind. He must be kept in his own abilities and capacities, both mentally and physically. You cannot relive your successes, failures or desires through your children. It is a sin to try and force your child to do what you want them to do… not what they are wired for. You will ruin them if you try. Let them be them, what God made them to be. If you keep them in prayer, God will help you know what they are destined to do.

Spend time with your children. That's how children measure love…T.I.M.E. Shut off the computer and the television. Listen to them; ***if you are talking – you are not listening.***

Watch for signs of what interests them. Start when they are very young, and then try to train them in their natural, God-given talents. Encourage them. You must be an encourager to them.

Everyone needs encouragement, especially children. If they falter, don't act like it's the end of the world, or a big bad thing. Don't put them down. Don't make fun of them. *Are you perfect?* And you've had a lot more time to gain perfection than your children. Do you ever make a mistake? Sure you do. Everyone does, and they certainly will. How you react to their mistakes will mold their self-images. It will ultimately decide how they treat themselves, others (you included), and God.

We don't sometimes attribute our own trials and tribulations to God's love. Often that would be hard to do. But consider this, IF God didn't love us, he wouldn't pay any attention to what we do. He wants us to grow in grace, wisdom, and stature. Job 5:17 says, "Behold, happy is the man whom God corrects: therefore, despise not you the chastening of the Almighty." Our children are the same way, IF we love them, we will correct them. In doing so, we show we love them and want them to turn out well.

There ae also at least two Scriptures that tell us to be consistent with our children, don' t be a flighty up and down parent. Ephesians 6:4 says, "And you fathers, provoke not your children to wrath but bring them up in the nurture and admonition of the Lord." Colossians 3:21 states, "Fathers, provoke not your children to anger lest they be discouraged." Anger kills productivity and discourages children.

NOTICE, these words are to fathers; don't break their spirits. Treat them as you want the Lord to treat you; gently and without malice

First Corinthians 13:11 says, "When I was a child, I spoke as a child, I understood as a child, I thought as a child: but when I became a man, I put away childish things." We cannot expect our little ones to think like an adult or act like an adult. They are not adults yet, and we are supposed to be…

A fast, violent, stubborn temper is a childish thing. Our children need us to be adults. They need to be children. Do your children have an adult in you to look up to? Someone who can understand their real – or imagined – problems, or crisis, even if there isn't one, without you going off the deep end and into a childish tantrum or violent rage? We may not recognize their problem as a crisis, but if they do, that is what matters. Are you going to teach them how to act in a crisis situation? If not, who is going to teach them how to react to a crisis – their peers, a liberal school teacher, a gang? Are we adult enough to meet their needs?

Many children, both boys and girls, join a gang for a family feeling…does your home have a family feeling? Or is everyone on edge all time?

What about your wife? Are you adult enough to realize the innate differences between men and women? Between you and your spouse? Are you able to accept and deal with her without rebellion? Without temper tantrums? One of the intrinsic differences between man and women is that she lives in the here and now, caring for the children the home, the things going on now. Usually the man is looking ahead into tomorrow, next month, next year, or ten years down the road. This is good. God made us this way to balance life. Someone has to be concerned with today, especially with children, but someone has to take care of the family tomorrow. See? It's good to be different. You each have a majority role to play, just different. We each must be careful not to look too much into today or too much into tomorrow, however, and neglect being aware of what is going on. Don't put her down for not looking ahead, she's a nester; God made her that way.

Contrary to a lot of women's cultic groups that say it is bad to be a "stay at home mom" or a "home engineer", that's the way God designed the family. It's the man's responsibility to support the family financially, and the wife's to take care of the home. If a couple divorces, it doesn't relieve that man's responsibility – in God's eyes - to take care of the family. Any 'Christian' man who is not paying his child support is not a Christian man, unless he is actually medically incapable of doing so. A man who is not supporting his family is denying the faith.

Christian divorces are sin – unless there are biblical grounds for it. It should always be discussed with your pastor(s) first to be sure the grounds are right. We know adultery is biblical grounds. I believe also that God does not expect a woman to stay in a home where the man is beating either her or the children.

How does a wife spell love? T-I-M-E! Time to love.

Titus 2 is a chapter on older people. For the men, it says (Titus 2:2), "That the aged men be sober, grave, temperate, sound in Faith, in charity and in patience." As fathers get older, they are to season. They should become more temperate, dignified, sensible, sound in Faith, in wisdom, in love, and in perseverance. They should become more "Christ-like" as the years add up, and example to all. Just as the older women are to teach the younger women, older men are to teach the younger men how to be husbands, fathers, and providers, men of God. And the younger men are to listen to and take sound advice from their elders.

Isaiah 28:16 is good advice for the older men and older women, a well for the younger fathers and mothers to strive for: "He that believeth shall not make haste." Are you running around like a chicken with its head off? Slow down, that's not right. We are to make haste to keep the Lord's commandments, but we are not to make haste in life's decisions. We should not make haste in any impatient or improper sense. Temper your decisions with understanding.

Charles Spurgeon wrote a phrase in the Salem Kirban Reference Bible that states haste very well. He called it "The Believer's Pace."

"He shall not haste to run away, for he shall not be overcome with fear, which causes panic. When others are flying hither thither as if their wits had failed them, the believer shall be quiet, calm and deliberate, and so shall be able to act wisely in the hour of trial.

He shall not haste in his expectations, craving his good things at once and on the spot; but he will wait God's time. Some are in a desperate hurry to have the bird in the hand, not likely to be theirs.

Believers know how to wait. He shall not haste by plunging into wrong or questionable action. Unbelief must be doing something, and thus it works its own undoing; but faith makes no more haste than good speed, and thus it is not forced to go back sorrowfully by the way which it followed heedlessly.

How is it with me? Do I believe, and am I therefore keeping to the believer's pace, which is walking with God? Peace, fluttering spirit!

Oh, rest in the Lord, and wait patiently for Him! Heart, see that thou do this at once!"

(I love to read the wisdom of this man of God.)

Wise? Do you think yourself wise? Are you wise? Proverbs 4:7 says, "Wisdom is the principal thing; therefore get wisdom, and with all thy getting…get understanding." The first step in acquiring wisdom is to make sure you really want it, that you will strive to obtain it. It's not always an easy thing to achieve, but we are to exalt, promote, prize, and embrace wisdom. But be sure to get understanding with it. Proverbs is an excellent place to start gaining wisdom. Almost every subject in life is covered in this book. I suggest that you start a training session with your family in this book. You will grow and so will your family, in both wisdom and understanding.

Come, you children, listen to me; I will teach you the fear of the Lord. Who is the man who desires life, and loves length of days that he may see good?

Keep your tongue from evil, and your lips from speaking deceit. Depart from evil, and do good; seek peace, and pursue it.

The eyes of the Lord are upon the righteous, and His ears are open to their cry.

Psalms 34:11-15

So much of the Bible, God speaking to us, talks about how a man should act. Proverbs 20:3 instructs, "It is an honor for a man to cease from strife: but every fool will be meddling." This covers a woman too. Do you strive to be free from strife? The Word of God says that God is not the author of confusion (First Corinthians 14:33), but of peace. Do you create or eliminate confusion? Does your very presence say, "Peace be still?" "A righteous man who walks in his integrity, how blessed are his sons after him."

God tells us that in Proverbs 20:7. Are your children blessed because of you?

Children of the just man will have a much better chance to be free from sin. Children need earthly "heroes," ones with skin on them. How much better for Dad or a biblical character to be their hero than some violent or humanistic cultist off the television, from the sports world – chewing and spitting, off the Internet, or from a video game.

Politics. What about politics? Whoa! Politics…you don't want to get involved in politics? You don't think Christians should get involved in politics? God says you must!

Psalms 105:21 and 22 tells us the king gave Joseph the job of "binding up his princes and teaching his senators wisdom." Men are o get and keep control over the schools and senators! Yes, that's right. School problems are yours. You shouldn't think it's the mother's. You are the one ultimately responsible to God for the upbringing of your children. The word 'prince' in this verse in Hebrew is sar, which means a keeper or steward. At school, your children are under a keeper or steward, and you are responsible to keep control over the keepers and stewards!

Men are also to get and keep control over their senators and representatives. Men obeying God's orders are to be taking an active part in the development and curricula of the school system and of legislative matters. The men are leaving too much of the political system open and vulnerable to liberals, feminists and undesirables. Conservative women are really being beaten up on, while too many Christian men are just standing in the sidelines and whimpering, "I don't believe I should get involved protecting my children." They are leaving their wives to try and fight the good fight for them. *Hogwash! Poppycock!* That's wrong.

The Bible clearly says the men are to get involved. Our

system of training our children will not improve until the moral men of our society stand up, get involved, and say, "No! This is the way it is going to be!"

OCCUPY: Luke 19:13, Christ speaking, "Occupy until I come."
Webster's Dictionary: Occupy = "Take possession of; grab hold of, seize, control, And reside in as an owner."

Does this sound like *Jesus* doesn't want Christians in politics? On the contrary, He expects you to get involved. He expects all Christians to be involved.

An angel of the Lord appeared to Zacharias to tell him of the coming of his son, John the Baptist. Luke 1:12 to 17 tells about the prophecy:

> And it is he who will go as a forerunner before Him in the spirit and power of Elijah to turn the hearts of the fathers back to the children, and the disobedient to the attitude of the righteous; so as to make ready a people prepared for the Lord.

In referring to the same prophecy from God, Malachi 4:6 said, "And he (speaking of John the Baptist) shall turn the heart of the father to the children, and the heart of the children to their fathers, lest I (God) come and smite the earth with a curse.

God is very stern with fathers that don't do their duty a God ordained.

Fathers...Who needs them? The answer is clear. We ALL do. We need them for strength, guidance, encouragement, training, correction, and buffering. Most of all, we need them for love, to set the tone of our homes and our lives. As the eagle flies under its young to keep them from falling, so the family needs the father to undergird them, to make them secure.

Fathers, you are the cornerstone of your family and the wind beneath their wings, just as Christ is the cornerstone of the church.
It's an awesome responsibility, being a father, and that's only one of the reasons God gave you the ability to reinforce the woman who is ruled by her heart, and the child who is ruled by his/her impulses.

Be still right now before the Lord. Think about your role as a father, perhaps one of the most important roles in the world. Can you think of says you can temper yourself to be more understanding, a better listener, speaking without sarcasm, better at recognizing the frailty of your family, and lead it softly until *Jesus* the Christ comes again?

Women, **caution:** It is a grave thing for a woman to let anyone come between a child and its father's godly teaching, correction or love. And that means you too!!!

Feelings

There is no right or wrong to feelings! Let me repeat, there is no right or wrong to feelings. They are feelings; that's what they are. Don't try to make them right or wrong. You can't! We all feel differently about different things.

I really want to drive this home. You cannot judge someone by his or her feelings. They are just feelings, not facts.

Women tend to be more controlled by emotions and feelings, generally, more than men, because they are normally ruled by their heart. So, men, if you are a guy who tells a gal that her feelings are stupid, then you are the one who is actually stupid. You don't know what you are talking about and are just rattling off at the mouth to feed on someone you *think* is weaker than you. Your ego craves putting people down. If you don't understand how *God made her,* you should be studying the Bible more instead of being a blabber-beak and making yourself look like an idiot.

Hold it, gals. This goes for you too. Don't prove yourself stupid by degrading anyone's feelings or lack of knowledge on any given subject. You also need to understand the man's 'feelings' of not understanding yours, because he feels with his head and not his heart, generally. That's the way *God made him.*

I have feelings. You have feelings. Everyone has feelings – especially children. Oh yes, small children have very tender feelings. Have you ever thought about that? Are you considerate of other's feelings, whether you think they are right or wrong? I'm not stupid and I hope you are not either Even when I 'feel' someone's feelings are wrong...I try to understand where they are coming from. Sometimes in the realm of looking stupid, we open our mouths and remove all doubt…

Christ *Jesus* is touched by our feelings. He loves a contrite heart and gentle spirit. He doesn't love a contrary heart, out to prove everyone – but y0u – is wrong! *Jesus* recognizes how real they are to us, and gives His grace in our times of need. Will you set yourself up above Christ *Jesus* by calling someone's feelings stupid? Probably not a good idea. They don't have to be facts…they are feelings.

Where are this person's feelings coming from? What made them feel like they do? This is what you should be asking. If you 'feel' their feelings are misguided after listening to them carefully (you learn more with your mouth shut), perhaps you can gently suggest an alternative. You are not the final authority; the Lord *Jesus* Christ is!

You have no right to be the "Big Chief" over anyone else's life. This does not please God. God isn't finished with them yet… and hopefully not with you either. We are to deal with others in all humility and kindness. The old phrase, "Do unto others as you would have them do unto you." This verse is from Luke 6:31, in the Bible, and it is a good motto to live by.

Perhaps you are saying that I am being unkind or showing lack of humility. Wrong! I love each one of you even having not met you yet, and I want you to ponder my feelings of truth. This is how I feel. I want to see each one of you in the rapture/resurrection (same meaning), and I feel God wants me to speak my feelings in this book. That's why I call it Thoughts Aplenty because this is what they are: my feelings. My trying to reach people and make them think. **We become fools when we let others think for us.** You may not agree with my thoughts or feelings, but if I can make you think and study, preferably the real Bible, then this book of my thoughts is worth all the work that has gone into it. I have a 'right' to my own feelings, and you do too; so does that person you feel is exhibiting wrong feelings.

The Apostle Paul tells us in First Thessalonians 5:21,"Prove ALL things; hold fast that which is good."

The Apostle Luke also tells us in Acts 17:11, to the noble people of Thessalonica, "in that they received the Word with all readiness of mind, and searched the Scriptures daily, whether those things were so." Commit these Scriptures to memory so you won't be misled.

Satan is walking to and fro about the world, seeking whom he may devour. We must press into the Lord and His Word to avoid the Slewfoot evil that he wants to do in our lives. (First Peter 5:8.) Don't be dinner for Satan. He is master at playing with our emotions and feelings; that way he can control us.

Give the devil a stomp. That's what I taught the children to do when I conducted Children's Church a few years ago. It really did make them stronger. We even practiced the *'devil stomp',* so why don't you try practicing it? Satan is under our feet. Stomp him!

Be constructive, not destructive, with feelings, no matter whose they are! That's what they are – feelings – not facts.

The Flag of the United States

I am the Flag of America.
I am the Flag of the United States of America.
My name is Old Glory.
I fly atop the tallest buildings.
I stand watch in America's halls of justice.
I fly majestically over institutions of learning.
I stand guard with power in the world.
    Look up and see me.
    I stand for peace, honor, truth, and justice.
    I stand for freedom.
    I am confident.
    I am arrogant.
    I am proud.
    When I am flown with my fellow banners
    My head is a little higher,
    My colors a little truer.
    I bow to no one!
    I am recognized all over the world.
    I am honored – I am saluted.
    I am loved – I am revered.
    I am respected, and I am feared.
I have fought in every battle of every war
    For more than 100 years.
I was flown at Valley Forge, Gettysburg,
    Shiloh, and Appomattox (1865).
I was there at San Juan Hill,

In the trenches of France, and
In the Argonne Forest.
I was on the beaches of Normandy,
Anzio, Guam, Okinawa, Korea,
And Khe Sanh, Saigon, Vietnam know me.
I was there.
I led my troops. I was dirty,
Battle worn, and tired,
But my soldiers cheered me,
And I was proud!
I have been burned, torn, and trampled on,
In the streets of countries
That I have set free.
It does not hurt, for I am invincible.
I have also been soiled, burned, burned, torn, and
Trampled on in the streets of my country.
And when it's done by those
Whom I've served in battle, it hurts
But I shall overcome, for I am strong!
I have slipped the bonds of Earth
And stood watch over the unchartered
Frontiers of space from my
Vantagepoint on the moon.
I have born silent witness to all of
America's finest hours.
But my finest hours are yet to come,
When I am torn into strips and used as bandages
For my wounded comrades on the battlefield.
When I am flown at half-mast to honor my soldier,
Or when I lie in the trembling arms of a grieving parent
At the grave of their fallen son or daughter,
I am proud!

Author unknown.

Hero-Trees

I somehow can see the parallelism between a tree and the Sermon on the Mount found in Luke 6: 17-49, and Matthew 5, 6 and 7. This is sometimes referred to as The Great Sermon, which it is, the words of our Lord *Jesus*, The Christ, to teach us how we are to respond to others and to ourselves. Following his words will lead you into a right and holy relationship with Him as well as with others, especially your family.

Fathers are special people. They must wear many hats. When God made man and woman, he made them alike, yet very different. A man usually looks down the road to catch and ward off things from striking his family (although some men cannot see the end of their noses).

A woman *usually* looks at the here and now. That's why she has the babies; she can keep track of six kids, the home, and a demanding husband. The man is stronger from the waist up than a woman. This isn't to flaunt his "beautiful body"; it is so he will be able to protect and provide for his family. Fathers are heroes. A child, especially a boy child, looks more in the hero line to his dad. When you hear a little boy brag, it's usually,

"My dad can beat up your dad." I don't suppose you'll very often hear him say, "My mommy can cook better than your mommy." Dad is usually the hero of the house. This is normal and good. Early on, a child recognizes the usual physical strength of Dad over Mom, even to having to open that jar of pickles Mom can't get open. I've seen little boys believe they have become a man when they could open the pickle jar Mom couldn't.

Just as a tree must have strong roots to survive, Dad, as the "family hero" you must also have strong roots for your family to survive.

Dan Quayle was and is right, the family is the backbone of our society, and when the family falls apart, thee Nation is doomed. So, as the Hero-Trees, dads must realize that a pupil will be like his/her teacher! Your characteristics will be carried on, especially in your boys. Plus, your gentleness and devotion will help keep your little girl from the throngs of an aggressive lion cub or worse.

Baby see, baby do; baby hear, baby say. What are they seeing? What are they hearing? If the teacher does evil, he will destroy life. If the teacher does well, he will heal and feed life. Good trees produce good fruit. Bad trees produce bad fruit. What kind of a tree are you? What are you teaching your children? Your children belong to God. You only have them for a while, and you will be responsible to God as to how you train them and treat them! God owns them for eternity.

Let's examine the similarities between a tree and Christ's great sermon. Turn in your Bibles to Luke six. I have it all underlined in my little blue Bible.

I love my little blue Bible so much and have used I for so long that it was falling apart. My husband, who doesn't even know how to sew on a button, decided to make me a new cover for it as a Christmas present a few years ago. He got some bright blue sailcloth - blue is one of my favorite colors – cut it up, and actually "sewed" it on my sewing machine. He made me a beautiful Bible cover that I use all time and treasure greatly. He did a Hero-Tree act just for me. How precious! Just for me.

<u>Love</u>: the 27th verse of Luke six, "Love your enemies, do good to those who hate you." Live is like sap running through you, Hero-Tree. Sap touches every part of the tree, bringing life.

Ephesians 5:2 says, "Walk in love, just as Christ loves and gave himself for us." Just as love covers a multitude of sin, tree sap covers injuries to a tree to help it heal. Are you your family's sap?

<u>Joy</u>: the 28th verse of Luke 6, says, "Bless those who curse you, pray for those who despitefully use you." Show the love of the Lord even through bad times. It is said - a sorrow shared is a half of a sorrow – but a joy shared, it twice the joy. Joy can cover the hard times, just as leaves cover the tree to protect its delicate branches and fruit. Are you your family's leaves?

<u>Peace</u>: the 28th verse of Luke wants us to be at peace with others. "Whoever hits you on the one cheek, offer him the other also; and whoever takes away your cloak forbid not to take your coat also.

Matthew 5:5 says, "Blessed are the meek: for they shall inherit the earth." Gentleness brings about peace. However, do not mistake meekness as being weakness. Moses was meek, but he was not weak. Meekness means patient and without resentment or malice. It does not mean a sissy or a weak person! Some of the strongest people you may ever meet will be meek, but they will be completive, they will complete things they start. Usually, if you need something important accomplished, give it to a meek person.

First Peter 3:4 that God considers a meek and gentle spirit

a great price. It is precious in the sight of God. It is also precious in the sight of our families. If a tree has a rigid trunk and it will not bend in the wind, it will break, causing the whole tree to die. Too much rigidity in a trunk can make an ugly tree. Many seedlings often come up from the roots left by the breaking of a rigid trunk, but they have no sense of direction, no purpose no plan, and most will perish.

Proverbs 15:1, says, "A soft answer turns away wrath, but grievous words stir up anger." Let your little seedlings see your gentle strength with other, and especially with them and your mate. How you treat your mate will have an enormous and lasting effect on how they view what marriage is. Is it solid? Is it caring? Is it committed? Is it peaceful? Is it gentle? Is it protection? You, Dad, set the tone of your home. You are the Hero-Tree. Your so will treat his wife just like you treat his mother. Your daughter will take abuse from her husband, and other men, it you give it to her Mom. Are you your family's 'safe haven', their place of security? In a father's arms, a child should have the world by the tail.

Long-suffering, Ephesians 4:2, "With all lowliness and meekness, with long-suffering, forbearing one another in love." Help to bear your family's burdens, help them to buck the elements of this world. Help them learn to be strong.

Ecclesiastes 7:8 assures us that, "Better is the end of a thing than the beginning thereof: and the patient in spirit is better than the proud in spirit." If we hang on until the end – we will reap our rewards with God. The elements can produce dire effects on our families. A Hero-Tree needs to be able to take what comes at the whole family and buffer it, just as bark buffers the inner workings of a tree's being. You need to be able to take things in stride, work through them, and let your sapling pupils see how to bring things to completion, even when it takes a long time or is difficult. Are you your family's buffer?

    Gentleness: Luke 6:31, is "The Golden Rule,' and the "And as you would that men should do to you, do ye also to them likewise." If you, Hero-Tree, want a gentle family, then you must be gentle with them.

    Proverbs 12:3 warns us, "A man shall not be established by wickedness: but the root of righteousness shall not be moved." Hold your temper. Don't take it out on your family. Your families are your seeds. They must be watered by gentle rain. They will sprout in good soil. Don't kill your family with your angry temper, with too much trunk, and not enough, sap, leaves, and branches. Remember, your wife and kids are seeds, your seeds, which Almighty God has given specifically to you for only a season. Their growth and development will be mainly growth from your actions. How you garden and care for them. Are you a loving gardener?

    CONSIDER THIS: *You are the one who provided the seed for your children…your seed fertilized the mother's egg. Without your seed, your children would not be here.*

    Goodness: Luke 6:32-33, "If you love them which love you, what thank have you? For sinners also love those that love them. And if you do good to them which do good to you, what thank have you? For sinners also do even the same." Goodness should be a fruit. Your goodness and righteous living will produce fruit in its season, at the right time. Your offspring believe in you, Hero-Tree, and need your cultivation to produce good fruit in its season. It could have a long-term, negative effect on your sapling if he or she sees you return evil for evil. Are you a good example to your family?

If you do good to those who do good to you, what credit is it to you? Even sinners do good for each other. The lessons your seeds will most remember will be the lessons of not returning bad deed for bad deeds. Be the bigger person, and rise above them.

<u>Lending</u>: Luke 6:34, And if you lend to those of whom you hope to receive, what thank have you? For sinners also lend to sinners, to receive as much again." Don't do something with the thought of 'what's in it for me'…EVERYTHING you have belongs to God, and if you are selfish and self-centered with it – God just may take it all away from you. God expects us to help others without expecting anything in return. Your saplings are watching you. Are you teaching them to be stingy or giving? Are you teaching them to tithe? Are you teaching them to be stingy with God Almighty? Do they know everything you have belongs to God already, and He is just letting you use it? The tithe you give back to God is already His. He doesn't really need His money back; He needs your obedience. Tithing is part of being obedient. Your saplings are watching you Hero-Tree.

<u>Faith</u> must be your root system. Roots soak up nourishment and faithfully pass it on knowing it will sustain the whole tree. The more you are into God's Word, the more nourishment you will be able to soak up and pass on to your family. If you have faith and follow God's Word, you will become sons of the Highest, and that is what every Hero-Tree should be striving for.

Be ye likewise a gentle Hero-Tree.

I Feel Lousy

Heavenly Father, I feel lousy this morning, and very honestly don't even want to read your Word. Please forgive my carnal attitude and open my mind that I may see wonderful things in your Word today.

NOTE:

     Read the Word when you feel like it…and when you don't…read it until you do. You will find that as you read, your "feelings" will gradually change, and you will get a special blessing from His Book.

Liberty??

Do people around you see you as "spiritual?" What an awesome responsibility!

Do you really realize your accountability to God concerning those people?

Perhaps you had better take a moment to reflect, calculate, verify, and count the cost you are going to have to pay when you meet *Jesus* Christ face-to-face on judgment day.

First Corinthians 8:9 says, "But take heed lest by any means this liberty of yours becomes a stumbling block to them that are weak." Read and reread this passage; commit it to memory! Christian liberty is not to be abused, not for your sake, but for the sake of others. If by our example we cause a weaker one to stumble or act in contradiction to what God's Word says…we are responsible.

Also consider verse 12 in this same chapter, "But when you sin so against the Brethren, ye sin against Christ." To cause a weaker one to 'fall' in any capacity – is to sin against Christ *Jesus*.

Whoa!! Are you sinning against our Lord by your liberty?

Think. Do people see you as 'spiritual'? Is everything you do okay in their eyes? Do they feel it's all right to do if you do it? If you drink, and your weaker brother or sister knows you do…this makes it not a sin in their eyes. You soak up that sin as a sin against Christ.

Getting drunk is a sin. Does your spiritual sister or brother – or someone you've been trying to turn to the Lord, see you light up a cigarette? Your liberty now tells your weaker brother or sister, or that unsaved one, that it is okay to smoke. After all, you are spiritual, and whatever you do must be all right. What are you teaching weaker people? You soak up their sin; you have caused him or her to stumble because they trust you. They are a weaker vessel. In teaching them wrong, you have sinned against *Jesus* Christ. How dangerous! How selfish!

Any habit is an idol, something you put before the Lord *Jesus*! If you have a drink, you have a lack of submission to Him. If you have to have a cigarette, you have an idol and are not truly submitted to Christ. Perhaps you need to get help to release you from this idol. ANY habit – even caffeine, pop, chocolate, shopping, television, telephone or computer (a bad one; many people are actually addicted to the computer) – if you must have it, it is an idol and shows your lack of submission to the Lord in that area.

Oh, I do love chocolate, but I don't have to have it. I really like my morning cup of coffee, but I don't have to have it. I can survive without it! You can survive without that crutch too.

What about a vile temper? That's a biggie. A vile temper is a total lack of commitment to the Lord, and there is no excuse for a vile temper – even if an unloving spouse, relative, or friend sets you up. It is totally selfish and self-serving. If you let your temper run out of control, then you are an abomination to our Lord, you are a sinner, selfish and spoiled; and God is going to purge you hard. You have an evil heart of unbelief, because if you were a believer you would obey God! Get right with God right now!

A commitment is a very serious thing. Is yours sincere? Are you really committed to Christ? We are bound to fail; only *Jesus Christ* was and is perfect. But we have the joy and peace of knowing we are forgiven when we fall, and not continuing in sin as a way of life. Read Romans 6. Every single Christian needs to read this entire chapter. It deals straight out with sin and forgiveness. No sweet covering…just the facts…Read the entire chapter – it doesn't take very long. If you continue in sin, make it a way of life, you are probably not saved, and you do not know Christ. This is such a good chapter if you are addicted to anything. Read and reread it, memorize it; it's only twenty-three verses.

A cigarette is not a heinous crime; it won't send you to hell, but it does create a stumbling block to the weaker vessels. They may progress from a simple cigarette to marijuana or to snort cocaine because they have not the strength of Holy Spirit working in them. Is that stick of weed worth it? Is that vice of your worth thee walk of your sister or brother with the Lord? What does it do for your testimony? Do you have any idea how bad you smell? The stench gets imbedded into your clothing, your hair (it cannot be washed out, it has to grow out and be cut off), and how may would be friends will shun you because you smell like a dirty ashtray? I'm asthmatic, and cannot be around anyone who smokes. Are you inflicting medical problems on your family?

Matthew 7:21 states flatly, "Not everyone who says unto Me, Lord, Lord, shall enter into the Kingdom of Heaven; but he who does the Will of My Father which is in Heaven." Christ actually tells those who do not obey in His own words, "Depart from Me you workers of iniquity, I don't know you." (Verse 23)

"It is a fearful thing to fall into the hands of a Living God." He is just and shall judge His people. (The ones who expressed their submission to Him, then have fallen away.)

In First John 2:3-4, we are told we know him IF we keep His commandments. ("And hereby we do know Him – if we keep His commandments. He who says; I know Him, and keeps not His Commandments is a liar, and the Truth is not in him.

Do not fall back in sin. If you do, you probably were never truly saved, you went through the motions…but your heart wasn't sincere. God looks on the heart.

Are you really committed?
Are you really spiritual
Are you really saved?
What is your trail?

Love Test

Do you really love your mate with the love of Christ? Study this and openly discuss it with your potential mate before marriage.

1.   **Vision.**   What is your vision? Is your vision the same as your mate's?

>   Do you know your mate's vision?
>   What is it?
>   What is yours?

2.   **Commitment**. Are you really committed to your mate? Think of the worst scenario you can. Will you still remain committed and faithful?

>   What's the worst?
>   What would you do?
>   What would your mate do?

3.   **Benefits.** Are you willing to give up immediate benefits and gratifications for the long-term benefits of you both?

>   What are the long-term benefits?
>   What can you give up to help?
>   What can you accept to help?
>   What are your long-term goals?

4. **Relating**. How do you relate to your mate? Are you aware of how your mate feels about any situation? Are you willing to discuss his/her feelings without getting angry or indifferent?

> What do you disagree on?
> How can you settle it?

5. **Words.** Is what you say to your mate degrading? Do your words encourage or discourage your mate? If your words do not encourage and uplift your mate, they you are selfish? If either of you degrade each other, DO NOT MARRY!

> What do you say to degrade your mate?
> What does your mate say to degrade you?
> How can you both stop the degradation? (This MUST be done before marriage; it _will eventually kill_ all love between you. And it must be done before marriage.)

> God hates couples picking on each other…JUST STOP IT!!!

6. **Empower**. Are you empowering your mate and allowing him/her to be an individual, or are you selfishly trying to control your mate? YOU are not his/her boss. Control is selfishness and SIN! He or she is not your slave or subordinate.

> How do you try to control your mate?
> How does your mate try to control you?

> Talk about it nicely. Come to an understanding. Even put it down on a "Do Not Do" list if necessary and both sign it. Your mate belongs to God, not you, and you are not to control him/her, that's for God to do!

7. **Esteem.** Do you try to build up you mate's esteem, or do you tear him/her down and criticize your mate at every move? Is he/she always wrong? Do you think you always know better how to do or say something than your mate does? Who made you God? You have no right to criticize your mate! His/her actions are not up to you. They are between him/her and God. He is a jealous God, and you might be putting yourself into the hands of an angry God. That's not a place you will find peaceful. Plus, don't you every try to criticize your mate in front of anyone. That is just plain and diabolically evil! Keep your mouth shut if you can't say something nice to your mate. *God is listening to every word you say!*

> What do you say to continually put your mate down?
> What does your mate say to continually put you down?
> What are you going to do about it?
> What is your mate going to do about it?

Perhaps you both need to put this on your "Do Not Do" list too, and both sign it. If your mate treats you with disrespect…it will not improve after marriage when   he/she does not have to be on good behavior…

8. **Enjoyment**. Has your spouse lost his/her enjoyment of life? How much of this loss have you caused?

> What do you do to make some fun for your mate?
> What are you going to start doing to put fun into your lives?

9. **Confidence.** Has your mate lost self-confidence? Is it because of your badgering and put-downs or from your snide remarks? Did you forget that your mate is God's property – not yours? Are you ready for the wrath of God? I'm sure not!

What can you do to be nicer to your mate?
What can your mate do to be nicer to you?

Apologize to each other right now, and ask for forgiveness from your mate…and from God.

10. **Success**. Is it all for your mate to succeed – or does any success intimidate or threaten you? Do you get jealous if you don't get the credit that your mate does? Get over it! God is the King, not you! You should rejoice if your mate does something deserving of praise, which is a good thing.

How will I stop being jealous of my mate?
How will I honor him/her for their success?

11. **Gossip.** A BIG one. Do you always speak well of your mate behind his/her back? Do you allow others to speak ill of your mate? If you speak ill of your spouse behind his/her back or allow others to, you are a creep. Male or female, you are a real jerk!

God is listening to you talk about His property, and He ain't a happy camper! Don't forget Hebrews 10:31, "It is a fearful thing to fall into the hands of an angry God." Watch out, you are in dangerous territory.

Do you need to ask your mate for forgiveness for talking ill about him/her behind their back?

Do it now, tomorrow might be too late. And, don't rat your mate again!

12. **Spendthrift.** Are you causing fights and problems in your marriage or relationship because you don't know how to manage money? You spend too much? Wastefulness is SIN. The Bible

says so in Romans 13:8, *"Owe no one anything but love."* Are you putting your family in debt? That is totally against Bible teachings. We are not to be in debt. If you don't have the money to pay for the merchandise, don't buy it. Medical emergencies are another story. Sometimes they must be charged because they are enormous. But that's all you should be charging. Stay home if you don't have the cash.

Clothes, nice things, eating out, etc. are not to be charged. Stay home if you don't have the cash.

Don't try to be Mr. or Mrs. Big Shot! God hates debt and a haughty spirit. The Debtor is a SERVANT to the Lender or Credit Card company. You cannot serve two masters. Either you serve the Lord, or you serve the credit cards. If you charge something out of state, and pay the card off completely when the Statement comes, then I think you will be okay if the purchase was not so extravagant that you cannot pay it off. Many times, in traveling, companies will not take a check, some will not even take cash anymore, so you have to use a card. Just be sure to count the cost before you travel so you will have stayed in budget. (I was floored the first time I ran into a company that wouldn't take cash…)

Never have over one charge card for emergencies. Don't shut God out and be someone else's servant, because that's what charging 'things' does to you. When you are not paying all the colossal interest costs, you will usually have pocket money. Proverbs 22:7 says, "The borrower is servant to the lender." In the Greek Text – used here – the word servant is *'Lavah'* meaning that the borrower actually joins themselves to the lender as their servant. To repeat for memory sake – Don't shut God out and be someone else's servant – that's what charging 'things' does.

I believe it is all right to owe for a home mortgage because it is an investment. God took the talents from the one who didn't invest them and gave them to the one who did. This is good as long as you be sure your home is an investment. What that means is that IF you keep the property in good repair, so the value doesn't decrease (Not withstanding a City-wide property value decrease beyond your control.), it will remain an investment. But, it you do not take care of the property and let it become dilapidated…it is no longer an investment…and God is watching. This means that as long as you keep it up; this means clean free of junk, painted, repaired, and yard trimmed, and looking like something belonging to God, it is an investment. If it becomes run-down, it becomes a sin to owe on it because it is no longer a viable asset, but a liability.

What can you do to help your finances?
What can your mate do to help your finances?
Do you have the guts to cut up all but one credit card – just for emergencies?

Do it NOW…especially any department store charge cards! Those are completely unnecessary, and not at all honoring to God.

Is the Lord satisfied or grieved by the way you treat the mate he has given you? He is watching you. God does not hear sinners.

Saint John 9:31, *"Now we know that God hears not sinners; but if any man be a worshipper of God, and does His Will, him He hears."*

Is God hearing your prayers?

My Prayer

I give this day to you,
Oh Lord, my God.
I give this day to you,
Oh Lord, my God.
Please take this day,
Control it your way.
I give this day to you,
Oh Lord, my God.

    I give my will to you,
    Oh Lord, my God.
    I give my will to you,
    Oh Lord, my God.
    Please take my will,
    Control it your way.
    I give my will to you,
    Oh Lord, my God.

        I give my praise to you,
        Oh Lord, my God.
        I give my praise to you,
        Oh Lord, my God.
        It comes from my heart.
        I give my praise to you,
        Oh Lord, my God. Amen

Ornaments of Easter

Do you enjoy the Easter ornaments such as rabbits, hot cross buns, eggs, and the resurrection of our Lord? I do. However, I keep the Easter celebration in perspective.

If you can keep the fiction separated and just enjoy the pastel colors of the season, not being completely swept up into the egg and bunny syndrome, then I think it is all right to enjoy Easter festivities. Children of all ages enjoy pretty colors, hunting brightly colored eggs, and eating those delicious chocolate bunnies. I like to color eggs all pretty and eat them later too.

Easter is a pagan holiday. In fact, the word Easter comes from ancient Babylon. Easter was the wife of Nimrod, the priest and king. Her name was actually spelled Ishtar, and was pronounced Easter. Babylonian folklore asserts that Ishtar, or Easter, claimed that she was given the 'promised seed' by her dead husband, Nimrod. Nimrod became the Sun-god when he died, making Ishtar the blessed mother, and she was to be worshipped as such. Her son, Tammuz, was worshipped too, as the son of the Son-god, and was symbolized by a golden calf. In fact, you would be put to death if you refused to worship either one.

Perhaps if we keep in mind that the Yugoslav people mark their eggs with X V, which stands for "Christ is risen," we can keep things in perspective and be sure that our reason for even remembering this holiday is to celebrate the resurrection of our Lord and Savior, *Jesus* the Christ. He came out of the tomb and is alive and well and will greet us at the resurrection/rapture of His faithful church. (Rapture and resurrection are the same word.)

The following are some of the legends for the various symbols.

1.   **Egg**: An egg of wondrous size fell from heaven one day and landed in the Euphrates River. Some equally wondrous fishes managed to roll the egg to shore, whereupon several doves descended from heaven and incubated the remarkable find. Soon, out popped Ishtar (Assyrian Sammu-Ramat or Greek Semiramis), the goddess of Easter. The egg eventually became the universal symbol for fertility and the symbol of the goddess herself. There are many legends about this person, and no one knows the truth. But the egg was derived from her many legends.

The egg became the symbol of resurrection because they hold the seeds of life and represent the revival of fertility upon the earth. Satan has cleverly counterfeited truth with an insidious lie. Old Slewfoot always counterfeits anything someone might enjoy; That's one of his ways of sucking people into his vicious web.

Another pagan legend is about how the universe originated from an egg. Among some peoples, the "Heavenly One" once inhabited an egg, which he broke in pieces, creating the earth in the process.

Still another: an egg split in two pieces, with one-half becoming gold and the other half silver. The gold elements became the sky, and the silver elements became the earth. The center membrane became the atmosphere, the veins became rivers, and the fluid became the oceans. (Just about as stupid as evolution.)

No legitimate connection exists between any such legends and the resurrection of The Christ from the dead! God created the heavens and the earth, not from some broken egg!

2. **Rabbits:** Everyone knows that rabbits don't lay eggs. But the relationship between these two Easter phenomena is indisputable. To be perfectly correct, it is the hare, not the rabbit, which should be honored as the most famous secular Easter symbol.

Easter is a movable feast, dependent for its date on the phase of the moon, and from antiquity, the hare has been the symbol for the moon. The rabbit is not.

Hares are born with their eyes open. Rabbits are born blind. The Egyptian name for the hare was "un" meaning "open" or "to open," and the full moon watched open-eyed throughout the night. According to legend, the hare was thought never to blink or close its eyes, thus a constant watcher of the moon. Hares are timid, long-eared mammals and are furred at birth. The rabbit is naked at birth.

3. **Easter Lily:** The fragrant, waxy, white flower is neither a spring flower, nor an American flower at all. A lily growing on islands near Japan was taken to Bermuda and then traveled to the United States to become our most special Easter plant. Flower growers have learned how to make it bloom on time. The Easter lily has long been revered by pagans of various lands as a holy symbol associated with reproductive organs.

I love the Easter lily plant. It is beautiful to look at, and smells wonderful. Besides, God made the Easter lily for us to enjoy. As long as we keep it in perspective, as just a lovely plant that the Lord has given us, it is certainly all right to enjoy it. God gives us many wondrous things to enjoy!

4. **Hot Cross Buns**: These date back to the ancient pagan custom of worshipping the "Queen of Heaven" with offerings of cakes marked with her image. It is said that the Egyptians made buns with two horns on them to offer to the moon goddess and that the Greeks changed the symbol to a cross so the bun could more easily be divided. Anglo-Saxons marked theirs with a cross to honor the goddess of light.

Jeremiah 44:17 & 19, talks about making cakes to the Queen of Heaven (Ashtoreth or Astarte. She was married to Baal/Molech called the King of Heaven), as a form of worshipping her. The prophet tells us the story of Ishtar and how the people were giving her homage. Even the brilliant Solomon supported the worshipping of Ishtar by drinking her offerings and eating her cakes.

The Hebrews in Egypt recognized this as a cult, but they argued in verse 17 that at least now they had plenty of victuals, or prosperity. Jeremiah told the people even in the streets of Jerusalem, that the Lord could no longer bear their evildoings. And, because of the abominations of idols, their land would be desolated; a curse, and without inhabitants.

Get the picture? God does not like idols!

The items were not evil themselves. But meanings attached to them can be. Stay balanced and keep things in proper perspective. (There's that word again: perspective.)

5. **Ham:** Ham for Easter is an English tradition, expressing, of all things, "bigotry toward Jews." Jewish people do not eat the meat of pigs – ham – to make it "the feast of the day" is a slap in the face to Jews. They still believe it is an unclean animal. Even if we believe the New Testament says all foods are clean, although they

may not be good for you, we should respect the beliefs of the Jewish people and not flaunt it in their faces.

The Jewish people are God's chosen people, and you had better be careful what you do to them, or you might incite the wrath of the Almighty! God has brought judgment on people and nations for not sticking up for His people. Are you aware that God brought WEATHER JUDGMENT 41 times in The Bible to those who tried to divide Israel or didn't support her.

Legend says that Tammuz was worshipped during the spring when the lilies were in bloom, that he was slain, and his mother, Easter/Ishtar, wept so hard that Tammuz came back to life again. The pagans incorrectly thought the resurrected Tammuz caused the arrival of vegetation in the spring. Of course, we know that only our God brings the spring and the fruits.

So, by all means, enjoy the spring season. Enjoy the ornaments of Easter, but be informed so you will be more able to remember the real reason for the spring celebration – because we really are celebrating the "resurrection day" of our Lord *Jesus* Christ, not some fable or goddess.

When speaking of the special day, I like to use Resurrection Day, not the pagan word: Easter.

I am so blessed to have a committed Christian husband, who knows the pleasures in remembering why we celebrate certain days. A man who can enjoy a Sunrise Service on Resurrection Day, and still have fun coloring eggs.

If you are dating, or possibly engaged, to someone who doesn't understand the wonderful things of God and the true meaning of the holidays born-again Christians celebrate, you are unequally yoked. Get out of that relationship now! You cannot change that person, no matter what they do or say. Sadly, you won't find out how he or she was just trying to impress you with their 'holy' actions until you are in a mess. His/her actions are the best now that they will ever be. It is much easier to pull someone off of a table, than to pull someone up onto a table.

That is why our Lord says, "Do not be unequally yoked." Second Corinthians 6:14. It is for our own good, to keep up from missing out on the many blessings that we can share only with a Christian mate. And, to prevent a bunch of heartache that always follows not adhering to God's Word.

The unsaved cannot understand or appreciate the differences between Easter and Resurrection Day, and they usually couldn't care less – or even want to know. It's just a holiday to them, for fun. As with most holidays, a good share of the people enjoying themselves without a single thought as to "the reason for the season." They think it is only for the enjoyment of the Ornaments of Easter.

Our God Is An Awesome God!!!

Several years ago, I received this from a friend. I don't remember whom, but it has lingered with me as ponderable and praise to our God for who He really is. Near the end of this "poem," it says to pass it on, and so I am.

> He is the First and Last; He is the Beginning and
> The End.
> He is the keeper of Creation, and the Creator of all.
> He is the Architect of the universe,
> And Manager of all times.
>
> He always was,
> He always is,
> And He will always be…
> Unmoved, unchanged, undefeated,
> And never undone.
>
> He was bruised and brought healing.
> He was pierced and eased pain.
> He was persecuted and brought freedom.
> He was dead and brought life.
> He is risen and brings power.
> He reigns and brings peace.
> The armies can't defeat Him,
> The schools can't explain Him,
> And the leaders can't ignore Him.

MARIE GRACE

Herod couldn't kill Him,
The Pharisees couldn't confuse Him,
And the People couldn't hold Him.

Nero couldn't crush Him,
Hitler couldn't silence Him,
And the New Age can't replace Him.
No one can explain Him away.

He is light, love, longevity, and Lord.
He is goodness, kindness, gentleness, and God.
He is holy, righteous, mighty, powerful, and pure.

His ways are right,
His Word is eternal,
His Will is unchanging,
And His mind is on me.

He is my Redeemer,
He is my Savior,
He is my Guide,
And He is my Peace.
He is my Joy,
He is my Comfort,
He is my Lord,
And He rules my life.
I serve Him because
His bond is love,
His burden is light,
And His goal for me is abundant life.
I follow Him because,
He is the wisdom of the wise,
The power of the powerful,
The Ancient of Days,
The ruler of rulers,
The leader of leaders,

And the Sovereign Lord of all that was, and is,
And is to come.
And if that seems impressive to you,
try this on for size:

When I fall, He lifts me up.
When I fail, He forgives me.
When I am weak, He is strong for me.
When I am lost, He is the way.
When I am afraid, He is my courage.
When I stumble, He steadies me.
When I am hurt, He heals me.
When I am broken, He mends me.
When I am blind, He leads me.
When I am hungry, He feeds me.
When I face trials, He is with me.
When I face persecution, He shields me.
When I face death, He will carry me Home.

He is everything for everybody, everywhere,
every time, and in every way.
He is God, and He is faithful.
I am His, and He is mine.
My Father in Heaven can whip
the father of this world.
So, if you are wondering why I feel so secure,
understand this:
He said it, and that settles it.
God is in control, and I am on His side, and that
means all is well with my soul.

Every day is a blessing, for God Is.
Pass this on if you mean it.

- Author Unknown

I love the Lord and thank Him for all that He does in my life. Therefore, I am passing this on to you. Yes, I do love *Jesus*; He is my source of existence and Savior. He keeps me functioning each and every day. Without Him, I would be nothing! But with Him, I can do all things

-- Philippians 4:13

Please Forgive My Hurt

It is often easier to forgive others than to forgive ourselves. Think about that for a moment. Are you angry with yourself for something you have done either to someone else – or to yourself? Although 'self-forgiveness' is not found in the Bible, it is a measure of common sense. It doesn't delineate between who you should and should not forgive. It says "FORGIVE"… I believe that includes ourselves. To not forgive ourselves is actually setting us above God, because He has forgiven us. The Bible does say to sanctify and cleanse ourselves in many places. You cannot sanctify or cleanse yourself without forgiving yourself. Don't let people use a 'play on words' with you. You must forgive yourself to sanctify, justify and cleanse yourselves.

Self-anger can manifest itself in many ways; it can make you cry, angry, or even violent. Anger can be very quiet and passive – or loud and obnoxious. It might also put you into another world, trying to escape from the present, and cause you to be daydreaming to the point you could put yourself, or others around you, in danger.

When you see someone loud, aggressive, and obnoxious, do you ever ask, "Why is that person acting that way? What has happened to this precious person to make him/her behave so inappropriately?" We are all precious in God's sight, including the unseemly one, even though God hates his sin temper. Yes, tempers are SIN when allowed to get out of control.

Ephesians 4:26 says, "Be angry and sin not: let not the sun go down upon your wrath." To do so is to give place to the Devil. There is a difference between a righteous and a selfish anger.

A righteous anger would be when you see someone getting hurt and you go to his or her defense.

A selfish anger is when you are mad at someone or something because you think you are a victim. We can usually only be victimized to the extent we allow ourselves to be. (That does not include children being abused or someone being kidnapped and beaten.) There is help 'out there' if we will just go for it. If you are involved in a God-fearing church, you have a Pastor and a congregation that will usually help you. Go to them with the truth. (If you have gone to them before with either a half-truth or a non-truth, they may not want to help you. Be truthful!)

When you see someone out of control, do you ever think that perhaps his or her home life is unbearable? Are they being brutalized either physically or mentally?

Often mental cruelty is much harder on a person than physical abuse. And harder to recognize. Why is this person so desperately seeking help not even realizing that their actions are quite possibly a cry for help?

If YOU are in an abusive situation – get out!!! God doesn't intend for you to be anyone's battering ram. You don't have to be subject to someone's vile temper for any reason; whether the angry person realizes why he or she is angry or not. Get out of that bad situation NOW or you become an enabler, and quite possibly a dead has been enabler. If you do not have anywhere to go, call the Police and they will tell you where shelters are located that will protect you.

Seek some Christian counseling for help if you can. Unsaved counselors – however eager they are to help – do not understand the things of Christ. But, you must first remove yourself from the explosive situation. After you leave, try to get the angry person to go to a Christian counselor also. As long as you are still living with the abuser…he/she will not get help. You must leave first – to get their attention. They are in strict denial, as you might be also. Most people who are abused have been convinced it's their fault… It's NOT – it is the fault of the one who is abusing you. Don't soak up that excuse-sin.

Young person, if you are dating someone and they exhibit a bad and critical temper – **_RUN_** as fast as you can the other way! Another bad sign is the potential abuser tries to isolate their victim. (That's a really bad sign.) Just consider – while you are dating that person – he or she is on their good behavior… Think of how they will act after they have snagged you, and no longer have to be on their 'good' behavior. YOU CANNOT CHANGE THAT PERSON!! It takes divine intervention…and YOU are not divine. Only God Almighty can change him/her.

A big thing to check out is – 'how does this person treat their Father or Mother?' That will be a good indicator as to how they will treat you. If a man is harsh with his mother, he WILL be harsh with you too. If a woman is aggressive and domineering with her father, she WILL be with you too. *After good behavior is no longer necessary.*

Inner anger can eat us alive. It can and will make us physically ill. It will cause our bodies to fail. Do you know that there have been people who have actually died from a broken heart? Grief can be a killer. Anger and unforgiveness don't usually hurt others; it hurts you. The person or persons who hurt you may not feel your pain, and sometimes they can find pleasure in your agony. That's right. A person with a propensity to masochism will find hurting you, little animals, or even big ones – or torturing a bug – or any other odd behavior, funny and pleasurable. That's right, they may even find it YOUR hurt and agony funny to watch. They might find it hilarious to watch your expression as they torture a bug. That is why it is so important to know who you are getting mixed up with; it could be a deadly relationship. <u>Do you want a masochist to parent your child?</u>

Our Lord *Jesus* knows how destructive and nonproductive anger and unforgiveness are. That's why He has told us in His Word so many times how to deal with these self-destructive feelings. That's right – ANGER is a self-destruction demon.

Oftentimes, when a person is told to pray, they smirk at it, saying they need real help. Let me assure you, our most powerful weapon against anger and unforgiveness IS prayer, talking to the Living God. We need to pray. In fact, prayer is so important that in First Samuel 12:23, God says, *"God forbid that I should sin against the LORD in ceasing to pray."* We need fellowship with our Creator; it can give us strength. If someone smirks at prayer – they don't know God!

Philippians 4:13 is one of my very favorite Bible verses, *"I can do all things through Christ who strengthens me."* Use Christ as a buffer. Fiery darts come at us from all directions. The ones that hurt the most are the ones that come from the people we love and trust. The ones we are not usually expecting. Your Heavenly Father will soften the ugly darts that life sends your way, but He will only help when you ask. James 4:2-3, *"Yet you have not, because you ask not, or you ask amiss."* Prayer is not a cop-out; it's a fact! Use Christ. He is always there for you. He will not laugh at you; He loves you.

Satan virtually enters the unsaved to torment them until they give in to hurting us. He cannot make anyone do anything they do not want to do! But he can torment them until they yield unto his vicious ways.

Luke 22:3, *"Then Satan entered into Judas."*

John 13:2, *"The devil put betrayal into the heart of Judas."*

John 13:27, *"And after the sop Satan entered into Judas."*

We must recognize and blame the source of evil. Satan! We cannot withstand Satan alone. The devil is as real as Christ *Jesus*. Me must keep the lines open with God, by way of prayer, to keep us safe. True, we do have our own wills, but we are not strong enough in ourselves to withstand Satan, but our God is! When we are using Christ, and walking daily in Him, we can have victory.

When people cure, assault or misuse us, or lie about or to us, betray a confidence, gossip, or stab us in the back, it's not always easy to recognize and blame the source and forgive the one Satan is using. We must learn to feel sorry for the poor, lost souls. If Satan is using you, you are not using Christ, and Satan is giving you a lying, one-way ticket to Hell.

<u>We must forgive others.</u>

Matthew 6:15, *"But if you forgive not men their trespasses, neither will your Father forgive your trespasses."*

Get it? You must forgive…or you will not be forgiven. However - forgiveness does NOT mean re-establishment of a relationship. You do not have to go back around anyone who has hurt you. There's a big difference between forgiveness and fellowship.

This forgiveness also includes forgiving yourself. Do you find it hard to forgive others? Do you find it even harder to forgive yourself? Do you even find it hardtop believe that God has forgiven you? He has! He tells us so in his Word, His letters to us, the Bible. Yes, the Bible is God's letters to us. But we cannot know what He is saying to us unless we read His letters.

Our Lord *Jesus* not only forgives us our sins, He forgets them completely…never to be remembered again - ever. Not even on judgment day.

Second Peter 3:9, *"The Lord is not willing that any should perish, but that all should come to repentance."*

Psalm 103:12, *"So far as the east is from the west, so far has He removed or transgressions from us."* This is the same as completely blotting out our sins.

Isaiah 43:25, *"I am He Who blots out your transgressions for My Own sake, and will not remember them anymore."*

Jeremiah 31:34, *"For I will forgive their iniquities, and will remember their sins no more."* This is speaking of His children, which we become when we accept Christ as our Lord and Savior.

See, when you are sincere and God forgives you   you are like a new born baby, without a past – never to be tried on your iniquities. What you do for Christ *Jesus* after you become a true believer will be the only thing you will be judged on at the Judgement Seat of Christ.

Think how it hurts when someone destroys something you made or love. God made all of us, and to lose even one of us to Satan hurts Him deeply. Your repentance must be sincere, and bear in mind that God can read your mind and heart and knows your sincerity. You cannot lie to God. It is stupid to try, and trying can bring you serious reproach.

Micah 6:13, *"Therefore I will make you sick in smiting you, and making you desolate, because of your sins."*

The judgment of the sinners will be awful. God will smite them with illness because of sin. This DOES NOT mean that all illness is from sin.

God expects YOU to have a 'sea of forgetfulness' too and not set yourself up above Him.

Many beautiful Saints get diseases, but this has NOTHING to do with sin. It just means that on occasion, God will use sickness to try to bring people to Him. God will use sickness for sin.

John 9:3, *"Neither has this man sinned, nor his parents."*

Illness is not a sign of sin…it's just life on the once perfect earth that man has made imperfect.

Satan cannot read your mind or your heart like God can. It upsets Satan when you are thinking about the Lord because he doesn't know what you are up to. Always keep old Slewfoot guessing. Keep in contact with – and use – Christ *Jesus*. If you are truly saved, Satan cannot enter you. God will not allow him to. If you truly belong to the Lord, in the name of *Jesus*, Satan is under your feet: stomp on him.

Have you honestly repented for your anger? What about your hurt? Oh yes, for your hurt too. Your hurt will ease when you ask for forgiveness for it, and that's a fact! I didn't realize that myself until a few years ago. Someone very important to hurt me badly. In fact, I was crushed. I kept talking to the Lord and forgiving her, but the hurt I felt wouldn't leave. It kept popping up to crush me more. It was affecting the way I acted, even keeping me from believing the Lord could use me. I felt I couldn't even serve Him. My hurt as letting, and keeping, me down, and I was letting down the Lord. I had asked God many times for help in getting relief from my hurt, only to turn around and pick it right back up.

When it's gone – it's gone!!! Forget it…it didn't happen… Don't think about it…don't talk about it…it's gone!

You must have a 'sea of forgetfulness too' or you are setting yourself up against God. Dangerous!! --- It's gone!!

I don't remember who said it, but when I heard someone speaking on forgiveness, Holy Spirit quickened his or her words right down into my spirit. I should ask for forgiveness for my own hurt? At first, I was perplexed. Why should I ask for forgiveness for my hurt? *I was the victim…* Right there was the problem…a Victim Mentality… Hmmm, indulging in hurt is selfish, self-centered and nonproductive. I finally, and genuinely, asked for forgiveness for my selfishness in harboring my hurt…for allowing myself to be a 'victim'… It worked! I really gave my hurt to God. I didn't want it back this time. It was gone. If we are truly a Christian – we are not a victim…

Perhaps you have a hurt in you. It is gnawing away at you. It is making you behave poorly, or putting you in hiding? Ask God for forgiveness for your hurt. Ask God to help you genuinely forgive those who have wronged you. Then FORGET it. Put it in your 'sea of forgetfulness' never to be remembered again. Don't has it up. It's gone. Leave it alone. Don't give it any recurring role. Stop being a victim. You cannot serve God and be a victim.

Satan will use your hurt and unforgiveness against you. He'll destroy you with it. Kick his ugly teeth in. Don't give him food to spit back at you.

Romans 12:19, *"Vengeance is **Mine** – I will repay, saith the Lord."*

Do you really think you could deal out better punishment than Almighty God?

You cannot defeat Satan without using Christ. Use Christ! He is our strength.

The PAST is called the PAST because it is the past. Leave it there. It's gone!!

Repeat out loud: "I can do all things through Christ who strengthens me!"

Remember it!
Use it!
Use Christ!

Pyramid Schemes Gift/Networking Programs

I hate pyramid schemes, and I'm afraid over the years several good people I know and love have been sucked into one. I know only the few that start the scam will benefit, but most will be ripped off. Where do people think this money comes from? How does the Lord feel about money schemes?

First, let me quote what Arizona's attorney general once said about pyramid/gifting schemes:

> A pyramid scheme is a fraudulent system of making money that requires an endless stream of new recruits for success. Recruits (a) give money to their recruiters, and (b) enlist fresh recruits to give them money. Gifting/networking programs are illegal pyramid schemes. Money is made by getting new recruits to join the program. In theory, each recruit's name eventually will be at the top of the "pyramid" as the new recruits are added to the bottom. At that point, the recruit expects to receive a multiple of the money that they "invested" in the gifting/networking program.
>
> The result of gifting/networking programs is inevitable – at best, a few people walk away with a lot of money, while most recruits lose whatever

money they put into the program. In fact, the only way anybody can make money through a pyramid scheme or gifting/networking program is if other people are defrauded into giving money upon a promise of getting something in return.

These schemes always constitute fraud. They use deception to get money. That is why they are illegal. They violate Arizona Law (Arizona Revised Statutes, Title 44, Chapter 11, Article 9, Sections 44-1735) as they involve recruiting people to recruit other people to recruit other people to recruit other people.

It is deceptive to claim to a new recruit that he or she will make money or even have a good chance of making lots of money. It is also deceptive to state that those gifting/networking programs are legal, as they involve a "gift", and that no one truly expects a return on his or her "gift." That is misleading and corrupt. Any scheme or plan that requires an endless stream of new recruits is fraudulent! There cannot be an endless stream of new recruits in a finite universe. The only honest claim one can make to the new recruits is that the odds are very great that they will lose whatever money they give up and that only a very small percentage of people will ever benefit from this scheme.

A typical gifting/networking program has fifteen slots: one at the top, two on the next level, four on the next level, and eight at the bottom. Each new recruit puts in money – typically $2,000 - and gets a spot at the bottom. When all eight are filled, the $16,000 pot goes to the person at the top. The pyramid then splits in half, with everyone moving up a level and the top person leaving the apex with everyone else's money. Now there are two pyramids, each with eight empty bottom slots to fill at $2,000 each.

While early participants are often able to receive their $16,000, the likelihood of later participants receiving money diminishes. Too many new participants are needed to fill the bottom slots. When there are no longer enough new recruits, the scheme collapses, leaving a lot of losers!

The Arizona Pyramid Promotional Scheme Statute (A.R.S. Statute 44-1731, et seq) prohibits any person from establishing, operating, advertising, or promoting a pyramid scheme (I'm sure most States have a similar Statute). Anyone who violates the statute is subject to *criminal* prosecution as well as civil sanctions.

Anyone who establishes, operates, advertises, or promotes a gifting/networking program is guilty of a ***Class 6 felony*** and can be subject to paying $10,000 per violation as civil penalty, restitution, attorney's fees, and all costs involved.

The attorney general's office *has* enforced the Pyramid Promotional Schemes Statute through lawsuits and enforcement actions in the past and will continue to do so in the future!

Anyone who has questions or information regarding the promotion of gifting/networking programs - or other pyramid schemes – should contact the State Attorney General's Office, Consumer Information and Complaints, in their state. I urge everyone to get available pamphlets from their Attorney General's Office on these rotten schemes, and be informed.

I've seen people who really couldn't afford it be ripped off and devastated after borrowing money to "buy in." They've wasted their food and rent monies, borrowed from friends and families and put themselves in a devastating position.

Unless you realize and recognize the usual tactics of a pyramid or gifting scheme, you will be easily fooled into becoming involved and become a victim, or causing another person to be ripped off.

Here is a typical example of how people get sucked in the fraud:

Someone invites you to go to a "business" meeting so you can hear about how you can earn lots of extra money fast…and it's all legal!! You go, believing everything is on the up and up, and that you may have just found that illusive way to invest for your future and retirement. Besides, your friend wouldn't steer you wrong. In a cordial, but usually harried, atmosphere, often surrounded by people you know are good and decent people, you are told this "opportunity" is a sure way of getting financially stable and to realize a fast and wonderful return on your "investment."

Smooth-talking organizers try to convince everyone that this "gifting" program is a fantastic shortcut to financial security. You will be told that in this "business" you don't have to pay large fees to get into the business, as you usually do; that you don't have to worry about keeping a large inventory of any products, that there will be no running around trying to find homes to deliver to. And you don't have to have any schooling or hassles. They make it sound like dream come true.

The main focus on the meeting will be the fact that all you have to do, other than investing the small amount of money as a "gift" ($2,000 is not a small amount of money to me), is to get others to join the "investment opportunity." The meeting will actually focus more on the recruiting of other participants than on selling the product of service. Why would anyone want to cause their friends to lose a big chunk of money?

Consider the results if one person recruited six new participants, and each of the six would, in turn recruit six others… Then carry the process through the nine steps to success:

1 - Starts pyramid

1.	6
2.	36
3.	216
4.	1,296
5.	7,776
6.	46,656
7.	279,936
8.	1,679,616
9.	10,077,696

At more than ten million people for every nine steps in the distribution program, the distributors soon would be recruiting on another. In order for everyone to profit in a pyramid scheme, there would have to be a never-ending supply of, willing, new participants. Obviously, there isn't. When the supply of any area runs out, the pyramid collapses, and most of the participants lose their investments (The Pyramid Graph courtesy of the Better Business Bureau of Arizona).

One thing that bothers me the most: it's usually the older people who are getting ripped off, those on Social Security or fixed income, already living on the edge. Oftentimes, they will take almost all of their savings and "give" it into the scheme, believing it will make them financially secure. It's a tragic situation when people are preyed upon and exploited – especially from those who were supposedly their friends. Those who exploit people are asking for- and will receive – the wrath of God Almighty!

The Medicare and Social Security Systems in our beloved America are in shambles, being robbed by people we have sent to the Congress and the Senate to protect us, but instead have sold us out and destroyed our earthly security.

People are frightened about their futures, and this is making even the very 'elect' fall for these get-rich-quick schemes. Remember the old saying, "If it seems too good to be true, it probably is!" We are not to be anybody's fool. We are not to rip, or be involved in, ripping anyone off, even if they will be so far down the line that you will never know them. That will never stand up in God's Supreme Court on judgment day – that you really didn't intend to clip anyone... We are to be informed. Greed is SIN!

Someone said pyramids are legal in Colorado. No, they are not. I called the Colorado Attorney General's Office and they said no they are not; they are illegal in Colorado. Don't be anyone's schmuck!

I heard that pyramids are legal in Florida. No, they are not. I called the Dade County Florida Department of Corrections, and a few years ago they arrested nineteen people in connection with a pyramid/gifting scheme. In Florida, the investment/gift was $1,000, with a promised return of $20,000. A vice-detective involved with the investigation noted that the ringleaders of the scams "cash out" early; that the rest of the participants are left holding the bag – and lose their investments. Among those arrested were schoolteachers, counselors, and professional people. This fraud reaches all walks of life. Don't get sucked in!

It's called gifting; however, why would you give someone you don't even know a gift of $1,000 expecting nothing in return? This is a stupid assertion. It's ludicrous to believe that you would just give a stranger – or even a friend – a $2,000 gift for no reason. Why would you? It's really exaggeration to say you are just going to give someone a bunch of money for no reason. If you give someone a gift in this sham, you are expecting something in return! Otherwise, you wouldn't have given a "gift" in the first place. Don't try to bleach it. It is shady at best, and you are a Christian? How dare you mock God! Counterfeit Christians will be a dime a dozen running around on earth after the rapture/resurrection (same meaning in the Greek)? Who or what is your God? What or who is your idol?

There are so many Scriptures in the Bible telling of God's displeasure with shady angles and get-rich-quick schemes. Many people who profess God on the outside have an evil heart of greed on the inside. God will say to them, "Depart from Me, you workers of iniquity, I never knew you!" Matthew 7:23. Ripping off anyone, no matter how far down the level it is, sin, and God will punish the sinner.

First Thessalonians 5:21-22, *"Prove all things; hold fast to that which is good. Abstain from all appearance of evil."*

Proverbs 28:10, *Whoso causes the righteous to go astray shall fall himself fall into his own pit."*

Proverbs 28:22, *"HE WHO HASTENS TO BE RICH HAS AN EVIL EYE."*

Matthew 24:24, *"For there shall arise false Christs and false prophets, and shall show great signs and wonders; insomuch that, if it were possible, they shall deceive the very elect."* These seducing spirits will lead many astray because of their love of money.
Get the picture People? Become informed. Don't accept things at face value, check them out!

A pastor and his wife that I had known and respected for over twenty-five years had fallen prey to this "gifting" scheme several years ago – people who should have known better. But it's hard to retire on a meager pastor's retirement salary. After more than fifty years of ministry, they must then live on the church mouse income. (I'm sure most of you have heard the saying, "poor as a church mouse.") It's not right, and that's how they got sucked in, and it was by another "Christian" they trusted. They have both gone to be with the Lord now. They actually weren't looking to 'get rich' – just add some income to their retirement.

I received a call from my husband at the time saying that the pastor and his wife wanted to get together with us for fellowship. We did this quite often, and I assumed we had another 'list' that needed fervent prayer.

Instead, the pastor told my husband that there was a meeting they wanted us to go to with them, especially me…he wanted my 'analytical' opinion. (They actually believed I am analytical- ☺). Believing it was a church function, I readily agreed.

Now this pastor had known for years that I am not interested in any get-rich-quick or pyramid schemes, and have always refused any sales pitches from anyone. It has always been a bee in my bonnet to have someone I thought was my friend approach me with a smile, making me feel like he or she were just glad to see me…then try to sell me something like a cleaning product, a new telephone service, cosmetics, or a 'gifting' program or --??

Some parties are okay, like jewelry or cosmetics, but mail a flyer to my home; don't accost me in public about selling me something. If, after prayer- yes – after prayer – I want to get involved I will call you with my confirmation. I try to never abuse my friends, and when my friends see me coming it's with a "What can I do for you today?" not "What can I do to make money off of you today?" Frankly, I've met people I would have liked to get acquainted with and perhaps become friends, but as soon as they were trying to scam me, I vacated the situation. The accosts were usually in front of other people who knew I have done financial counseling for years, thinking I wouldn't say no in front of them. Wrong, they really didn't know me too well, so it's good-bye; another one bites the dust.

Anyway, back to my "pastor story." I had been having a problem with an ocular migraine. I had never heard of them until I became a victim. When my husband called me from work to say we were invited to the "analytical" meeting, my eyes were just 'tired'. But by mid-afternoon, my eyes were hurting pretty badly, and the pressure caused me to take a nap with some Aleve for pain. I was sleeping when my husband came home. He was surprised to see me asleep because I never take naps. He woke me to see if I was alright. I told him I could not go to the meeting, so please make my apologies to our friends. He decided to go to the meeting anyway.

My husband is a very trusting person and honest to the core, which makes him gullible sometimes, and an easy target.

When David came home, he was all hyped up about this fantastic way to make some investment money. He started telling me about the meeting. There were several of our friends there, and only first names were used??? Right off the bat…that perked my antenna… I became suspicious. It seemed peculiar that at the meeting only first names were used. Why would people want to hide their identity? Wasn't this a group of Christians? And the company – if it were a legitimate company – wouldn't everything be up front and open? Skullduggery breeds in the dark…

And just before the meeting started, someone closed – and locked – the door - "so people could not journey in off the street and get the wrong idea about the money exchanged". Hmmm, this sure did trigger my curiosity! I guess it's a good thing I had a migraine to stop me from going…I might have made a spectacle...

The meeting hostess then thanked the people for coming and mentioned that a guy from the Phoenix Police Department had looked this deal over and said it looked legal. People stood up and gave their first names, what their businesses were, and then were asked to put their business cards on the table by the back door.

As David described the scene, I couldn't help but think that integrity went out the window. And, again I felt it was a good thing I wasn't there, I'm not afraid to call a scam what it is.

Everyone was put in lines of eight people. Each gave $2,000 in cash, counting them out in one-hundred-dollar bills, as they said to the recipient standing by the tape recorder, "This is my gift to you; there are no considerations, all taxes have been paid." This blew me away. I was flabbergasted. God is soooo good, He knew I should not be at that meeting, that is why He gave me the ocular migraine right on time.

David became uneasy seeing this pastor giving money away, and the doors being locked. He said he became just plain uncomfortable; that his spirit was checked, and he wondered if the police would bust in at any moment.

Why, if this was a gift, were they expecting something in return? A gift expects nothing in return. Why was this made a public spectacle in the giving? He reasoned that it was to draw in other people. I reasoned that it was so no one would "blab" on anyone else; they were all guilty. When he stopped and looked at the overall picture, it just didn't feel quite right.

After the meeting, my husband questioned the pastor's wife. She emphatically denied it being a pyramid scheme or anything shady. Then her countenance changed, and she became arrogant, and told him that everything is a pyramid – even the police department. Whoa! Wrong! The Police Department is a "chain of command." I told David so. He hadn't thought of that at the time, and really didn't know what to say to her outburst. So, he said nothing. But she had almost convinced him I was wrong.

People are told, "It's legal." But the average person does not check things out. Perhaps they don't want to know full truth. They want to know just enough to satisfy their own desires. Besides, these were Christians running the show! What do you think they are going to say – "This is a crooked scheme, you will lose your money. We want to take it from you and go on vacation?"

My husband was shocked to think that there were so many people who should check things like this out, but don't – even learned people. They get caught up into making money too easy. It's a big temptation; people are using people.

At that point, I knew for sure that this was a pyramid scheme, and I told my husband I didn't want to know anymore. I reminded him that he and the pastor and his wife had known without a shadow of a doubt that I would not get involved in a shady or illegal scheme. That it was a good thing I hadn't attended the meeting, because I would have disrupted it!

He called the pastor, and talked with him a while, and told him my view.

Then my husband became a bit defensive and indignant to me. He snapped that I probably didn't know what I was talking about. That, after all, these were mostly longtime Christians, and wouldn't get involved in anything shady. He told me I was just too quick to put down something I really didn't know anything about. He too was glad I was not at the meeting, as I would have embarrassed him and the pastor.

Satan is a deceiver, trying to fool even the very elect! And Satan had even put doubts in my own husband's thoughts. He knew all the longtime Christians.

Well, perhaps I do put things down too quickly, but I don't think so, but for the sake of argument, I insisted that we get our Bibles and see what the Bible says about get-rich-schemes.

We sat down at the dining-room table, and the Lord kept brining Scriptures to me. As I would say them out loud, we would jot them down so we could look them up. Several times, my husband would say, as I repeated one, that he recalled the same Scripture. God was filling us in. I truly needed God's wisdom at that hour because I was going to be going up against many seasoned Christians and pastors.

We made a list of several things out of the Bible.

My husband stopped by the pastor's home after work the next day. Neither the pastor or his wife would even look at what we had written. They didn't want to know. David said the pastor's wife's demeanor changed into someone he didn't even know. That's what the love of money will do to you! She really snapped at David. Their bizarre behavior startled my husband, and he came home really hurt and confused. Was I wrong? He questioned me again. He couldn't believe that two such wonderful people could be so wrong. People so smart and knowledgeable about the Bible, such longtime honest and godly people. I too was dismayed. I really felt betrayed that they would try to deceive me into going to a pyramid meeting.

With my husband having such a hard time accepting the situation, we went back to the Bible. Plus, I decided I should take another look at what the program was about just in case I was wrong. We trusted these honorable people, but my guts still said it was a pyramid, and the verse, "False Christs and false prophets will do such wonders that if possible even the very elect will be deceived," kept running through my mind. Matthew 24:24.

As we jotted a few more notes down, I took a look at my husband's actual notes from the meeting. I had seen the same little circles a friend of mine had approached me with about three months earlier. Exactly the same little circles. One on top, and eight at the bottom, with a $2,000 "gift' to get in. (Nothing less than a lottery – only lotteries in Arizona, and most elsewhere, are legal, even if not moral.)

I asked my husband to call my friend and talk to him. David did call him. Sure enough, it was the same scheme. The two of them talked quite a while; then our friend said he had gotten out of it. He said he had become tired of the pressure to bring in more recruits, and people begging him to stay in and put some of his earnings back into the pot. He hadn't won the big jackpot, but a much smaller one. The name of the organization was the same as the one my husband had gone to.

When my husband tried again to convince the pastor and his wife they got really arrogant with him. There became a tremendous breach in the relationship between our pastor friends and us. Also between another pastor friend and his wife, who had also been sucked into the scam. They were told of my opposition and remarks about the scheme and were very angry with me for trying to squelch a 'good' thing.

They all lost their money, as I knew they would. I felt really bad for them and urged them to ask God for forgiveness for letting Satan lure them with false hopes. That is all Satan ever does, gives false hopes so he can relish in our 'crashing'.

It can be so disconcerting to know that so many people of God, supposed wise, are foolishly falling for such a far-reaching scheme. Are they even considering those down the line from them that they are leading astray? How can the countenance become so affected by the love of money? How can people once enlightened in God's Word sanction such chicanery? People, you really must study the Bible. Answers to every question is in the Bible.

Another pastor's wife declined to be drawn into this same scheme, and they were calling her a bad guy too, even saying that she had a personal vendetta against them. How awful for her. She was trying to keep them from going to jail. Like me, she was worried what the media would do with the story – like blow it up royally when they found out that many Christians were in it, especially pastors. What were these Christians trying to do to other Christians? Had their consciences been seared?

Matthew 16:26, *What is a man profited, if he shall gain the whole world, and lose his own soul? Or what shall a man give in exchange for his soul?"*

Mark 8:36, *"For what shall it profit a man, if he shall gain the whole world, and lose his own soul?"*

Luke 9:25, *"For what is a man advantaged, if he gain the*

whole world, and lose himself, or be cast away?"

Pyramid schemes are an illegal operation. But even if it weren't, as a Christian, you would have to look at the morality of such a scheme. Something can be legal, but is it moral? Would *Jesus Christ* do it? He is watching you now – and what you are doing. Will what you are doing really hold water on judgment day?

Every Christian will appear before the judgment seat of Christ! To give an account of what you did after you became a Christian.

Proverbs 1:19, *"So are the ways of everyone who is greedy; which takes away the life of the owners thereof."*

The majority of the world, sadly, is "greedy for gain" and will do almost anything to get with they want…right down to murdering or maiming someone…But…ripping someone off is the same a murder in God's eyes. You can destroy someone with greed.

Proverbs 15:27, *"He who is greedy of gain troubles his own house;"*

Isaiah 33:15, *He who walks righteously, and speaks uprightly; he that despises the gain of oppression, who shakes his hands from holding of bribes,"* These are the Children of God. He takes honesty very seriously.

Second Corinthians 12:17, "Did I make gain off of you by any of them whom I sent to you?"

Have you? It is an evil and perverse time we live in, where even the very elect will possibly be deceived by false showings. Satan is running to and fro, seeking whom he may devour. Don't be a meal for Slewfoot. Pyramid schemes are hypocritical shams, and we must not get deceived into evil and unlawful schemes. Nor should we send anyone to a friend to make them a victim of any scam. We should be trying to protect our older people and not rip them off. They are so frightened and in a virtual panic by a future of uncertainty, mostly by the misuse of the Social Security monies they have paid into for so many years. The Social Security was to be monies that would take care of them in their "Golden Years." This is why they fall prey to so many evil schemes: fear!

Social Security coffers need to brought back up to speed, and refunded with monies we are giving away to our Enemies; and then put in a BOX so no one can touch or borrow from it again. It's not the government's money…it's the Peoples.

A good source of a company's honesty can be checked out with your local Better Business Bureau *free*. It is working for you, just like the Attorney General of your state. But they cannot help you – or the elderly – getting ripped off if you do not contact them.

These scammers know that most elderly people have their hidden 'nest egg' for emergencies…and they are doing everything they can to get their grubby hands on it.

God hates deceit! There are many, many verses in the Bible that talk about the judgment coming to anyone who rips anyone else off. I can list at least 38 verses in the Bible about money. I encourage each of you to read all the Scriptures you can find on money… - It just might save your soul…

YOUNG PEOPLE, REMEMBER THE BANANA,

WHEN IT LEFT THE BUNCH…

IT GOT SKINNED…

JUST A CAUTION TO YOUNG FOLK!!

REWARDING BAD BEHAVIOR IN KIDS

TEACHES THEM TO BE SELFISH, OBNOXIOUS,

AND REBELLIOUS. DON'T DO IT!!!

A WORD OF WISDOM TO PARENTS

Sailor's Letter Home

A friend of mine sent this to me and asked me to send it on to as many as possible. This proves that we have a "family" in all nationalities and colors. We never know what a wonderful experience we can have by entertaining "strangers."

This is an e-mail from a young ensign aboard the U.S.S. Winston Churchill (DDG-81) to her father. The Churchill is an Arleigh Burke Class AEGIS guided missile destroyer, it was launched on April 17, 1999, and officially commissioned on March 10, 2001. It is the only active U.S. Navy warship named for a Foreign national. The radar can guide more than one-hundred missiles at the same time to various targets. It's a powerful and amazing craft. It really gives you pride to see it. She weighs in excess of 9,200 tons and is approximately 509 feet long. That's a big one.

Anyway, the letter says:

"Dear Dad,

"We are still at sea. The remainder of our port visits have all been cancelled. We have spent every day since the attacks going back and forth within the imaginary boxes drawn in the ocean, standing high-security watches, and trying to make the best of it. We have seen the articles and photographs, and they look sickening.

"Beyond isolated, I don't think we appreciate the full scope of what is happening back home, but we are definitely feeling the effects. About two hours ago, we were hailed by a German Navy Destroyer, Lutjens requesting permission to pass close by our port side.

"Strange, since we're in the middle of an empty ocean, but the Captain acquiesced, and we prepared to render them honors from our Bridge-wing.

"As they approached, our conning officer used binoculars and announced that the Lutjens was not flying the German, but the American flag. As she came up alongside of us, we saw the American flag flying at half-mast and her entire crew topside, standing in silent, rigid attention in their dress uniforms. They had made a sign that was displayed on her side that read, "We Stand By You."

"There was not a dry eye on the bridge as they stayed alongside us for a few minutes and saluted. It was the most powerful thing I have seen in my life.

"The German Navy did an incredible thing for this crew, and it has truly been the highest point in the days since the attacks (World Trade Center). It's amazing to think that only a half-century ago, things were quite different. After Lutjens pulled away, the officer of the deck who had been planning to get out later this year, turned to me and said, "I'm staying Navy."

"I'll write you when I know more about when I'll be home, but this is it for now.

Love you guys."

Origins: The above-quoted text comes from an e-mail sent by an officer serving aboard the U.S.S. Winston Churchill, to her father in the days immediately after the September- eleventh terrorist attacks on the U.S. in 2001. It was accompanied by a photograph of sailors from the German destroyer FGS Lutjens holding up a banner reading "We Stand By You."

The above excerpts from the e-mail were posted on the U.S. Navy web site by the Navy Officer of Information 26 September 2001.

My mother always said, "The way to get rid of an enemy… is to make a friend of them."

Singing the Psalms

How many of you reading this book ever get frightened? I do. Is there someone or something you are afraid of? Do you ever cringe when someone comes close to you? Are you ever afraid to be in the dark?

You don't have to answer these out loud, but just think a moment about them.

Do you ever wish you knew some way to find peace when you get scared? There is! Just sing the Psalms. Psalms is a book in the Old Testament of our Bible. King David wrote seventy-three of these beautiful orations, including the Twenty-third Psalm. The Jewish people use the book of Psalms at their hymnal or songbook, and they sing praises to God from it. We can too!

The Bible says that God inhabits the praises of his people (Psalms 22;3). That means when you are singing to God you are asking Him to come close to you, and He will. It's that easy. Just sing to Him and He will come really close to you. Actually, the Lord never moves away from you; you only move away from Him. So, when you are singing the Psalms, you are moving closer to Him. It's a good thing to sing praises to God, our Lord and Creator.

The Lord reminded me not too long ago that He helped me get through some very difficult times by singing the Psalms right out loud. When you are singing out loud, you are calling God's Holy

Spirit close to you, and you are listening to your own singing. In other words, you can hear what you are singing. Remember that we become what we take in, whether it is food for our bodies or thoughts into our brains

As you are singing out loud you will find the peace of God will come all over you, the fear and fright you were feeling will begin to leave and you will start feeling better.

I love the Ninety-first Psalm. It is a prayer for protection, for security, and for the blessings of His love. It has sixteen verses and tells us about the angels protecting us in times of trouble, and about God being with us in in times of trouble and helping us get through them. It tells us how powerful our God is and to what lengths He will go to protect us. But, we must trust in God, and we must call upon his name when we need help. Talk to Him like He is right I the room with you – He actually is!

The Bible does not tell us that we will not have troubles! Don't fall into the trap that if you become a Christian your troubles will be over; it's just not true! Everyone on earth has - and will have – problems because Satan has control over the earth until *Jesus* Christ comes back physically. But it does tell us that God will be with us and help us get through our bad times. He knows how we feel. We just have to be faithful in calling upon Him when we are scared, weak, or tired. Our Lord and Savior, *Jesus* the Christ, walked on this earth for thirty-three years. He saw and heard everything. He genuinely knows what we are going through. *Jesus* has been there, done that, and seen that.

In His years on this earth, he experienced everything this world has to offer, even death. He knows how it hurts to be lied to, or about, or blamed and convicted of something He didn't do. He was innocent, and yet He allowed Himself to be crucified as guilty. He was 100% God, but he was still 100% man…He felt and hurt just like you and me.

His friends lied to Him.

His friends denied knowing Him.

He had His back torn open with the lictor's whip. Then He had to carry that heavy and splintery crossbeam for His own crucifixion on His bleeding shoulders. Can you try to imagine the pain involved doing that?

People that once listened to Him preach and teach love were now spitting on Him and actually tearing his beard out. Grab your hair and pull hard. You can control how much hurt you want to endure by just letting go. Now, think about Christ, who couldn't stop it as it was actually completely ripped from His skin…

Think about a hammer piercing through your wrists and ankles - a nail that had to be as big as a railroad spike to hold the victim on the cross. They weren't little 8-penny or 16-penny nails like we see today. These were huge spikes meant to hold several hundred pounds securely on the rough tree.

Can you just imagine the humiliation of being stripped completely naked at you are displayed for everyone to see? Pictures you see have a cloth around His privates, but this is only for aesthete – to not offend. And no one helped Him except for a man, who was compelled to help carry His cross by the name of Simon Cyrene. That was virtually the only help Our Lord got in his agony.

I'm not saying your problems are minimal, but do they compare to what our Christ went through for you - and for me? So we could have eternal life…

He knows exactly how you feel, how you hurt. Talk to Him, He understands. You don't need to worry about a fancy prayer; just talk to Him like He's right there with you. Actually, He is right there with you, and you don't have to talk fancy to Him. Just talk normal. He knows your heart. He loves you more than anyone else will ever love you. You can trust Him!

I'll bet most of you reading this book know the Twenty-third Psalm. It's called the Shepherd Psalm. This is a beautiful and special Psalm to sing aloud. It talks about God taking care of us through the valleys of hurt and sorrow. It only has six verses, so it is an easy one to sing. In fact, it's fun to sing the Psalms in different ways. Try opera, western, hillbilly, deep base, or tenor. God loves it when we play with Him like little children, the Bible say so. (Always keeping in mind - He is a Holy God.)

It can be fun memorizing the psalms. You can even have a friend join you in singing; then God can have double pleasure. One of you can do soprano and the other one bass, harmonizing. This will make you laugh, and will give a great lift in spirit, as well as draw you and your friend closer. It will make a three-cord bond that will not be easily broken. You, the Lord, and a friend made special.

Satan hates it when you are singing, especially to God. I believe that singing hurts this diabolic creep's ears. Just think, you can give Satan an earache. That alone should make you feel better. You can also give this dirty buzzard a "Satan Stomp" and hurt his feet. I find great pleasure in giving Slewfoot a headache. With my voice, that only God can love, it really torments this buzzard bait

Satan. I cannot sing, and on day I was cleaning the bedroom, and Big Kitty was lying on the bed watching me…and when I started singing…he got up and left. That's pretty bad!

But you don't have to have a magnificent voice. God gave you the voice you have, and He loves it. Hard to imagine it's beautiful to Him…and yours is too. Keep singing the psalms, and drive Slewfoot mad…

Do you know how much Satan hates the Bible? It tells of his destruction and the abolition of his evil works. That is why old slime-mold is trying everything he can to keep you from reading the Bible. He throws distraction after distraction at you. When you are reading your Bible, you become stronger, and you are learning to not be so afraid. Satan wants us to be weak and frightened; only then can he control us. He will try all sorts of disturbances to keep you from reading God's Word. He'll tell you that you are not 'in the mood' or have too many things to do right then, or you have to get ready for something important…or…or…or. He will put any excuse in your way than he can just to keep you from getting fortified. He knows where your weaknesses are, and what he used before on you that worked. He has to keep you weak to do his dirty work in your life. Reading God's Word makes you stronger, and even though you may have fallen for slime-mold's traps before…you can resist them this time…stop being his victim!

God acts on our prayers, and if we don't pray, how can we expect God to do anything? He answers our prayers, every single one, and if we fail to pray, he has nothing to work with, does He? He doesn't always answer our prayers immediately. Sometimes He says, "Yes," sometimes, "No," and sometimes, "Wait." But He does answer every single one in His omnipotent timing.

How many of you remember to pray when you are frightened? Sometimes if we don't even know how to pray about something, or are too scared, or tired, to think of anything eloquent to say, we can just keep repeating His name, *"Jesus, Jesus, Jesus,"* right out loud. There is power in the name of *Jesus*, and it's easy to say. As you are reading this, please say *Jesus* out loud. Again, *"Jesus."* Again, *"Jesus."* See how easy it is to say *Jesus?*

If for some reason you cannot say it out loud at any given time, just think His name, *Jesus, Jesus, Jesus.* Think His name over and over. *Jesus* Christ can read your thoughts. He also reads lips; you can just "lip" the word *Jesus*, He'll know.

Next time you are scared, or if someone is hurting you emotionally or physically, say, *"Jesus, Jesus, Jesus,"* either out loud of in your thoughts. Keep saying *Jesus* until you feel better or the danger is past. You have a free will, and *Jesus* will not intrude in your free will. That's why it is so important that you ask Him for what you want or need.

As soon as you are able, start singing the psalms again. You really will find comfort and strength!

Listen to the Twenty-third Psalm. I think this is King David's most beautiful song of trust. He pictures the Lord as the Great Shepherd who cares for and protects his sheep and as the One who provides for them abundantly.

Psalms 23:1-6,

1) *"The Lord is My Shepherd; I shall not want."*
   [The Lord is our guide protector, and constant companion.]

2) *"He makes Me to lie down in green pastures:*

He leads Me beside the still waters."
[Quiet or still waters can be found, He is our peace.]

3) *"He restores My soul: He leads Me in the paths of Righteousness for His Name's sake."*

[He restores us, bringing us back to peace and health through the provisions of food and water and through repairing our inner beings. God's leading is always in paths which are right because He is a Holy God, and He wants only what is good for us. He is the vine, I am a branch, and I will follow His teachings.]

4) *"Yes, though I walk through the valley of the shadow of death, I will fear no evil: for You are with Me: Your rod and Your staff they comfort Me."*

[The Shepherd protects his sheep with his rod or club to fight off Evil, and He guides us with His staff.]

5) *"You prepare a table before Me in the presence of My enemies: You anoint my head with oil; My cup runs over."*

[God provides all that we need. He will feed your soul so you will not hunger after peace, but will have it. Applying oil to your head is a sacred rite, consecrating you to Him. He is your source. Come and feast from His banqueting table.]

6) *"Surely goodness and mercy shall follow Me all the days of My life: and I will dwell in the House of the Lord for ever."*

[God's covenant and loving-kindness are forever. If we follow Him and call upon His wonderful name, we will forever be in The place where God lives: in the house of the Lord.]

Isn't that comforting? Doesn't it make you feel safe knowing that God will restore you and make you complete? You don't have to fear evil, for God Himself is with you. He will see you through whatever you are facing. Your heart can runover with the love of God if you will trust Him and talk to Him. Remember that you can talk to *Jesus* anywhere and at any time. If you are too afraid to talk out loud, remember God can read your mind and thoughts, so you can just think your prayers to Him and He will hear you. No one can stop you from thinking thoughts to *Jesus*! God reads lips!

You can even make up a song to God. He loves it when we make up a song especially for Him. That makes the Lord feel very special; His own song. It can be a sad song, a happy song, even a silly song, or a song about what is bothering you. Yes, you can even make up a song to God about what is troubling you, and He will listen. If you want to make God feel special, make up songs just for Him.

God loves you so very much. You must believe that. It's true! He wants to talk to you about your play, your work, your likes and dislikes. Talk to Him today. You will feel better, and your God will love it.

Sing the Psalms to your God, He will listen.

Singles Scene

Okay guys and gals, this is going to hurt. But I was in the single scene for years, and I know of what I speak. Hopefully my acquired wisdom will help shield you from some of the distress I went through. Please remember I write this because I love each of you in *Jesus*'s name, and I want each of you in Heaven. Check out what I am saying with the Bible. God loves you too, and His Word will talk to you if you will listen.

First, I want to embed this into your conscious and subconscious memory. It is vital!

IF YOU FALL IN LOVE FAST, YOU WILL FALL OUT OF LOVE FAST!!

So will the person you are falling in and out of love with!

A slow, caring, right, and godly relationship is the one that will build lasting, supportive, and sincere love. If you are in a relationship with anyone who doesn't want a right and godly relationship – it is never love, just lust. It will fade.

We are to always put our mate before ourselves. Their rightness with Almighty God should be a priority. If it is not – you are with someone God hasn't chosen for you.

John 14:15, *"If you love Me, keep My Commandments."*

John 14:21, *"He who has My Commandments, and keeps them, he it is who loves Me."*

Get the picture? If you love your Savior, you will keep His Commandments. Man's biggest problem is keeping the Commandments of God. A Commandment is not a suggestion.

Perhaps you need to review: Deuteronomy 5:7-21, before you continue and before you finish this treatise. It won't take you very long, and then you will know for sure that I am speaking right out of the Bible, *the absolute Authority!* As you read the Seventh Commandment think about what it is saying (verse 18), *"Thou shalt not commit adultery."* ANY sex outside of marriage is adultery. It's just that simple!

Do not push a relationship. When you do, you take it out of God's Hands. Our Lord *Jesus* didn't even start doing miracles until he was over thirty years old. There's no rush. Only a solid, slow start will be a firm commitment. Repeat that over and over until you convince yourself that Christ is right. Oh, there have been a few "fast relationships" that seemed to have stood the test of time, and have worked out fairly well, but it is not the norm.

If someone really loves you and wants a firm commitment, they will not do *anything* at all to your detriment. If they do, they are selfish. Consider this:

Selfish people get angry fast.
Perfectionists get angry fast.
Suspicious people get angry fast.

There is nothing that justifies a desire to hurt anyone, even your ex-spouse. *Jesus* rebuked Peter when Peter became angry in *Jesus'* defense. "Vengeance is Mine." Saith the Lord, "Not yours." (Romans 12:19)

Idol: Anything that captures our attention or time; a temporary thing. If that "new love" is above the Lord *Jesus,* then it is an idol, and not from the Lord. Christ is always to be first in our lives. Keep *Jesus* in His proper place, and if your new relationship doesn't like it – dump him or her. They are not from God. They are not your God-given soul mate. A God-given soul mate will be more interested in keeping you in a right relationship with God, than with their own feelings and/or lusts.

Keep *Jesus* first, He will not desert you at the first wind.

If you are in a relationship with someone who is telling you that you are engaged or planning on marriage and sex is okay… they are lying to you! *You are NOT married yet!* Sex outside of marriage is sin. If you think it is alright, then you probably are not even saved. You had better search the Scriptures to see of you are approved (Acts 17:11 and First Thessalonians 5:21-22).

If you are divorced, don't set yourself up for another failure. Take your time. Wasn't the first one hard enough? Do the right thing this time. If someone is truly committed to you, they will do the right thing by you. If not, they really do not love you or care what happens to you, including going to Hell with them for your sins. You are just a piece of discardable equipment. Don't be anyone's discardable equipment again! *YOU are too special and too important to Jesus.*

Don't turn down your Savior for lust, and that's all it is. Don't give up *Jesus* for a wolf in sheep's clothing (Matthew 7:15), but beware of those who want to use you. Anyone trying to convince you that adultery is okay is a false person – a liar!

First Corinthians 5:9-13, *"Do not keep company with a fornicator. Do not even keep company with fornicators. Fornicators are wicked people, put away yourselves from that wicked person, do not even eat with them."* If you are now in an adulterous relationship, stop. Get out of it. Ask God for forgiveness. Make things right with your Creator. Any sex outside of marriage is adultery, and will stop your blessings, and God will not look on sin. What if the rapture/resurrection happened today? Would you be left here on earth with your unholy partner? Do you really want to go to Hell? If the one you are in a relationship with won't agree with you to live within Christ's rules, then dump him/her. You are just a piece of meat they are enjoying. If they loved you, their first thought would be to keep you in a right relationship with God Almighty. It's both that person and Hell – or *Jesus* and Heaven. You cannot have it both ways. Either you are saved – or not! There is no middle or hazy ground. The Bible is clear and absolute.

Pastors, teachers, leaders – if there is a wolf in your group, oust him/her immediately. Get rid of them! Don't let them ruin or tear apart any others that you have watch over.

First Corinthians 5:13, *"Therefore put away that wicked person from among yourselves."* If you are leading a "flock," it is up to you to buffer them (You will be held responsible), especially single sheep. Most of them have come from a hurting background; they don't need a pouncing vulture to re-destroy them. They need honesty and truth – and rest.

If someone tells you, "Everybody's doing it, or it's just old-fashioned to remain pure, and that's for the olden days, we're in a new generation now. We live in a different culture now than when the Bible was written." Consider this, Christ said that some worldly traditions will try and make His Commandments non-effective, and called the perpetrators hypocrites. God never changes, and His Word is still valid.

Or what about this line, "God was tempting me, and I failed." NO, God tempts no one!

James 1:13-15, *"Let no one say when they are tempted, I was tempted of God, for God cannot be tempted with evil, neither tempts He anyone. But everyone is tempted, when they are drawn away by their own lust, and enticed. When lust is conceived, it brings forth sin and sin, when it is finished, brings death."*

No, God never tempts you, but Satan sure will. So never say you "just failed God's test." It wasn't God, it was Satan…and Satan won. Uncontrollable lust is Satan's passion.

Children? What about children in the single scene? Before you hook up with anyone, see how he/she relates to your children. Especially how they speak to, or not, of their own children. They will generally treat yours worse. See how he/she treats your children… That's the best it will ever get, since they are on their good behavior and want to influence you. They will be nicer to your kids now – than they will be after marriage. Think about it. If they are inpatient, ill-mannered, or selfish of your time now, it will get worse if you are stupid enough to marry them.

Can you feel tension when you are with this person and your kids are with you? Do you feel a slight tinge of jealousy even through the smiles and "show?" It will get worse.

You should not bring 'dates' to your home. Your children must be shielded from strangers until you know the new person well. Then and only then do they get the HONOR of meeting your children. The children do not need to see your conquests. What if they are a child abuser or molester? Be absolutely sure of who they are before your kids are exposed to them.

If your kids are unruly, that's bad, and it is up to you to correct them, not someone else. Shame on you if you let your kids rule the roost.

In the same manner, you should not be trying to correct other's kids. If they become unruly, tell the parent in private. If the parent won't listen, remove yourself from the situation, even if you have to take a cab home. IT WON'T GET ANY BETTER! If a parent will not correct his/her kids, it is not up to you to do it. But you do not have to be under the bad behavior of anyone's kids. You should leave, not try to punish them. It's not your place or right.

It would be proper to tell the parent – in secret – why you are leaving. Sometimes "a word to the wise is sufficient." But remember, he/she is on their 'good' behavior, and it won't get any better. If they don't correct their kids now, they sure won't after they catch you. Plus, you will live under constant tension. It's not worth it.

I once heard a ten-year old boy tell his father's date that "He controlled his father, so she might as well get used to it. He's the boss." That woman was stupid and married the man anyway. That sure didn't last…the kid had told her the truth…he was the boss and no matter what the lady said to her new husband…the kid over-ruled it…and this was supposed to be a Christian man…

YOU MUST REMEMBER, WHEN YOU ARE DATING… IT IS THE BEST IT WILL EVER BE!!!

God says IF you love your kids, you will correct them. If you cannot control them, go talk to your pastor, or a Christian counselor. I don't like psychiatrists, and if you go to them you just may have your kids taken away from you as an unfit parent…But there is usually an older lady or gentleman at your church that will do counseling. Ask for help. Oftentimes, especially when you are single, children will look at a pastor as an authority figure that they can trust.

The kids have been crushed by your divorce too, or even a death. They are totally insecure. Children need authority; it gives them security. But be sure your correcting is to train the child, not to make you feel good by punishing them for your anger. I've witnessed too many times a parent taking their anger out on their kids. Hey, idiot, the kids didn't cause the divorce, and they are hurting too.

Never teach your kids that adultery and fornication is okay by shacking up with anyone. Your kids are watching you and they feel it is alright if you do it; you are their example and whatever you do must be okay for them to do.

Never touch anyone inappropriately in front of anyone – especially your kids. It can make them think sex and affection is dirty. A pat on the shoulder is appropriate; a pat on the butt is not.
Never leave the training of your children to anyone else. YOU are responsible to God!

Never scream at your kids. This is a very foolish and selfish thing to do. It gives your kids the upper hand too. You are out of control if you are a screamer. Get some counseling fast. It is also where a lot of child abuse starts. In fact, screaming at your child is child abuse; I don't care how frustrated, tired, or harried you are. There's just no excuse. It is a bad habit. Break it!

As a single person, it is imperative that you watch your finances. You cannot keep up with Joneses, so don't even try. If you need something, let your need be known to your church and fellow Christians. Forget frivolous things for now, they are only temporary. Stop the Charge Cards.

Romans 13:8, *"Owe no one anything but love."*

Debt generally is sin, and most of it unnecessary. You don't need 20 pairs of shoes, and 10 handbags. That's extravagant. The money you receive for Child Support is NOT yours. Nothing of yours should be bought out of it…that's sin…that's stealing. It's for the kid's needs – not yours. Part of it can be used for food – because they do eat. Part of it can be used for rent or house payments – because they do need a roof over their heads.

You don't need 15 televisions. Get one nice one and leave it in the family room. Kids should never have a TV in their bedrooms. You don't need a brand-new luxury car. Granted you do need a dependable one when you have kids. But you really can't justify a Land-Rover. Now, the parent that doesn't have the children most of the time is morally bound to help with the purchase of a dependable car for the person driving the kids to school and all their doctor's appointments and activities. Just because a father or mother pays Child Support, that doesn't – in God's eyes – exonerate them from the responsibility of making sure their kids have what they need. Are you a Christian - or not? Do you believe God – or not?

Concentrate on the important things: your spiritual condition; your children's spiritual condition; the children's education; your continuing education if that is what is necessary to provide for your family. What are your children eating – or watching on TV? Keep up with the daily tasks of home life. Who are your children's friends? Who are your friends? What are you teaching your children? What are you teaching yourself?

Are you teaching your children how to handle money? Do you know how to handle money? Are you teaching you or children that if they "want" something it is alright to charge things on a Credit Card? It's not! You are teaching them to be irresponsible and not a survivor. You are teaching them to sin. The only time you should use a credit card is for a medical expense or an emergency. Not for clothes – nor "things."

You cannot buy your children's love and respect. In fact, false teaching them can ruin their lives – respect for you. Will they not know how to manage money because of you? Are you sending them down a road of worry and bill-dodging? Do you want them to fail? Do you need to get some Christian financial counseling on how to manage your money?

What about your lack of management skills, probably a major reason your last marriage or relationship failed. Were you a spendthrift? What about a miser? One is just as bad as the other. Were you too strict with your ex-mate on how much money could be spent? Did you forget that ALL monies belong to GOD and He is watching how you steward it? Did he or she have the freedom to spend a small amount of money if they wanted to without a long conversation or pleading? (However, large purchases should always be talked and PRAYED about, and agreed on, before the purchase.)

Did you make up a budget? Did you stick to it? Do you have any idea how important a budget is? It's not a waste of time. Do you know how important it is to have the children in on the Budget?

They need to learn how to budget too. Budgets build responsibility in both children and adults. I have witnessed instances where kids were not nearly so demanding on what they "wanted" when they knew they were on a family budget, and how the money had to be proportioned. Even young kids can understand what a budget is.

I've heard so many kids say, "Why can't I have that?" But when involved in the budget – they don't have to ask – they understand.

A "God Squad" can be formed that could help each other, and others in the church who need help, such as widows and handicapped people. Everyone would fill out a form saying what he or she can do to create a "God Squad" helps list. Then 'petitions' could be submitted to the group's leaders to be matched with those who would be able to help.

Babysitting time could be traded, thereby freeing mothers and fathers to have a bit of 'me' time, because they could be confident that their sitters were trustworthy.

A wiener/marshmallow roast would delight the children (and adults) while needs were being taken care of. Older children could handle the preparation of this.

Perhaps someone's water heater needed replacing, a room painted. An evaporative cooler needed cleaned and new pads and started. Carpets could be cleaned and windows washed, a favorite shirt could be mended. Quick and inexpensive recipes could be exchanged and explained.

I would truly like to see singles groups get together once a month to help meet the needs of each other. The ladies could learn to cut hair. The men could check out the ladies' vehicles, do oil changes, etc. Swimming lessons and First Aid training are very necessary. If the child's parent doesn't know how to swim or faints at the sight of blood, usually someone in the group knows how to teach swimming lessons, with the parent present, or mop up the blood and clean a wound. Mom or dad can learn too!

This would build camaraderie and security within the group. It would be all volunteer. However, water heaters, oil, etc., would have to be purchased by the one who needs the item, unless there is a "Helps Money Pit" where everyone who could afford it would contribute to the fund. With a "God Squad," the possibilities are endless for helping each other in a concrete manner.

I really feel like a group like this could alleviate the single getting too involved too soon with, perhaps, the wrong person. Everyone would have to be sure and not expect "something" in return, and be willing to pass the help along. When a person is lonely, they will often do things they shouldn't – just for companionship. Singles, be a good listener. You have two ears – and only one mouth. That means you listen twice as much as you talk. Don't be critical.

Single life can be very lonely. God did not create us to be islands. We need fellowship, like a little boy said in a story I once heard referring to the Holy Spirit, "I want someone to talk to – someone with skin on." That's why we become so vulnerable in the single life. We need someone to talk to who can know where we are coming from.

Be careful that you do not become a 'blabber-beak' or 'motor-mouth'. You need to listen to others too, as much as you need to talk to them. Repeat: Got gave us two eyes, two ears, and only one mouth. That means we should listen and watch twice as much as we speak.

If someone tells you their deep hurts and feelings, never betray their trust. They already feel betrayed…don't heap hot coals on them. They don't need more hurt. If you lose your credibility, you will lose all your friends. Honest people don't like their feelings aired or blabbed about in public by others. It is better to know the hurt of someone and not blab it. God hates gossip!!! Do you want Him to hate you? If you cannot keep the trust and secret of someone, do the right thing, and don't accept the confidence. It is better not to know something, than to blab it.

Ladies especially listen to this. There are perverts out there preying on singles, both men and women, but especially on you gals. Watch for signs of masochism propensity's. These people are dangerous. You or your kids could wind up dead! If you get acquainted with someone who seems to find other people's hurts funny – or seems to like to play too rough with animals – to the point it hurts them, or even enjoys torturing bugs – run! If they play so rough with children that it hurts their spirits – run! This person very likely has masochism tendencies, and in a fit of rage might cage you or one of your children You need a Hero-Tree that will gently lead your family on, not an extremely selfish person who doesn't care who he/she walks over – or hurts – as long as Mr. Big gets his jollies. PLEASE, I beg you, for your sake, and for your children's sakes, be sure anyone you connect with is not a selfish person. They are only Trouble, with a capital T.

The old saying, "If a man can get the milk free, why would he go to the expense of buying the cow?" This is true. Another one to keep in mind is, "Men sleep with whores, but marry chaste ladies." If you get in bed with anyone you are not married to, you are just a cow giving her milk free. The marriage bed will be healthy and fun if you save your milk!

Any single person getting acquainted with another single person, and who feels that the relationship might possibly develop into something deeper, must ask some hard questions – and watch for some hard signs.

1. Does he or she bad-mouth hers/his ex all the time? They are uncaring, and will do the same to you. It is a definite danger sign.

2. Can you talk with them matter-of-factly about his or her failed marriage or relationship? You should be able to, not just a passing acquaintance, but one you could really get serious with. If a person is "over" the past and ready to get on with the future, they won't become defensive about their past and refuse to talk about it. Those who are defensive, and even angry, just are not as committed to the new relationship as you are.

3. Can you talk up front an honestly about your finances, debt, how you handle money? How heavy a person's debt load is will certainly tell you what you could be in for if you were to marry this person. Money is a very important topic in a marriage; it has caused many of them to fail. Every household should be on a budget. I truly think money problems, more than anything else, is the cause of marriages breaking up.

The "engagement" period is for bringing all things to the forefront. You should be using actual figures in making up budgets and personal financial statements. Every Christian should be making up a Financial Statement at least once a year. The Bible tells us to know the condition of your finances. If this "other" party is a heavy spender and deeply in debt, he or she will drag you down into the mud too. Better to know now than when it's too late, and you are already married.

If he is flaunting a big boat…ask him where he got it, and if it's paid for. If she's sporting a $500.00 handbag, ask her where she got it, and if she paid for it with cash – or a credit card…

<u>If their previous marriage failed because of money…yours will too!</u> Unless he/she received in depth Bible counselling.

4. Who will handle the family checkbook? Of course, you both pray about your expense together. But one should have the job of paying the bills.

5. What is their method of correcting children? Do they believe in corporal punishment or just time-outs? What leniencies to they think children should have? Anything they want? All name brand clothes? All thrift store clothes? Are they allowed to stay overnight with someone else? Can they have a friend stay overnight with them? Do they have a curfew? Are they force fed if they don't like what is fixed to eat? Bedtime? Study time?

Allowed time on the computer? Allowed time on television, restricted shows? We must never allow children to become "couch potatoes" because their grades will drop, and they will lose interest in life around them. They cannot be allowed to live in the television. What shows can they watch? What shows can they not watch? How about household chores?

Allowances? What chores are just "family" chores and which ones are paid ones? There is a difference, you know. Putting their dishes in the sink or dishwasher in not a paid chore; it is a family chore. You must decide how much allowance each gets, and for what. All children should get different amounts of allowance. That's right, people! Children get allowances for what they do, and older kids have to do more, so why should a four-year-old get as much as the ten-year-old who does more work? They shouldn't. AND,

IF they do not do their chores – they do not get their allowance!!! That is teaching them that the world owes them something, and they do not have to accept responsibility for what they do. They will become leeches. Don't take away their desire to better themselves.

Don't make your kids like cattle, all the same. Each one is uniquely different; treat them differently so they will learn to respect differences in people.

All of these "kid" questions need to be thoroughly discussed before marriage. If these things are not settled before marriage between you two, **without the kids around,** the kids will realize fast that they can play you against each other. Then the children have the absolute control over your home and your marriage. Children must never be in "charge or control" of any household. You parents must remain in absolute control. To allow a child to control the home is a recipe for disaster. You will be training up a loser!!

Like little computers, we become what we take in. You and your children are like sponges; you soak up the bad along with the good. It's important to stay involved in a spirit-filled church under pastors who speak the truth, instead of massaging people to get better offerings.

I have lots more to say about the single life. It is hard. I know only too well. But there is one thing I want to add, and I earnestly caution you. Bury this deep in your heart and mind.

No one ever loved someone and drug him/her into immorality!!!

That is not love; it is only lust. And God will punish you!

You must keep God the center of your attention. When you do, everything else will fall into place, at the bad you encounter will fall away with truth.

Be right with God – not the world.

Then, "Ye shall know the truth, and the truth shall make you free." John 8:32. **_Luv U!_**

Thoughts for the Day

1) We must forgive people; even when they are self-centered.

2) We must be kind; even when we are wrongly accused and our motives questioned.

3) We must be aware that being successful will bring false friends as well as true Enemies. Strive to be successful anyway.

4) We must remain honest and frank; even when people cheat or speak ill of us.

5) We must remember that even though we've spent many years building something, it might take seconds for someone to destroy it. Keep building anyway.

6) When we become as content and serene as possible while on this earth, we may experience the wrath of jealousy from others. Keep happy and positive anyway.

7) We must remember that people will quickly forget any good you do today. But keep on being and doing good; it's The Lord's way.

8) Always give your best, even though it may never be enough. Always remember, you are actually giving to God anyway.

9) In the end, life is between you and God, not 'them' anyway.

Train Up a Child – Buts

FIRST and foremost, NEVER argue with kids; this gives them control over you!

Following are some "Buts" you might be using to keep from doing what's right:

1)   "*But* I have three kids. How can anything – furniture, books, toys, or clothes – stay in good condition?"

Teach them respect for other-people's property. Never borrow anything unless you return it in the same, or even better condition than when you borrowed it. This goes for the kids borrowing things too.

2)   "*But* I work outside the home."

So did I. So did my mom – and she was a single mom WITH SIX CHILDREN. She cleaned houses and did ironings to support us. *We knew what we could and could not do.* Now it would be called "child abuse," but my mom took the bristles of a broom to us. She weighed only ninety-seven pounds soaking wet, and all six of us kids were husky. The broom was her equalizer. And guess what, not even one of us got on drugs, or was ever in prison. We were not allowed to be couch potatoes…we had an old basket-ball and football, and we had to go outside and play. Get exercise. Exercise is good for the brain.

3)   "But my spouse doesn't help me much, I have to do everything by myself."

Again, my mom was a single parent. She, like lots of people, didn't even have a spouse to help at all. Shut off all telephones and televisions when you get home. Pay undivided attention to your kids. Turn on your answering machine so you can return calls later. They might not like not having any telephone or television in the evenings, but they WILL get used to it. And you all will get better acquainted.

4)   *"Bu*t mine are boys, and they don't listen too well."

That's your fault. You don't enforce what you say to them. Perhaps you are a 'nagger.' My mom had two boys and four girls. She would tell us once; the second time the reminder came in the way of straw to our backsides, where God put the extra padding for the correcting process. If you are a screamer, or a nagger, what else can you expect? You are teaching them disrespect for everything.

5)   *"But* I don't believe in corporal punishment."

Poppycock. So, you believe your kids would be better off to be druggies and prisoners? You would rather they lost their souls? You don't know the Bible!

Proverbs 10:13, *"But a rod is for the back of him who is void of understanding."*

Now verse is NOT talking about an actual piece of steel. <u>In the Greek, it is a "Shebet."</u> A Shebet is a branch or stick called a scion. So, when the Bible is referring to the ROD of correction it is actually the scion of instruction. Not a steel rod of any kind. The bristles of a broom are really good scions.

Proverbs 13:24, *"He who spares his rod (Shebet/scion) HATETH his son; but he that loveth him WILL chasteneth him."*

Got that: IF you love your child you will correct them. Now, there is a big difference between correcting and child abuse. If you are guilty of child abuse, you are evil and have no part in Heaven! If you are not evil, just misinformed or out of control, you will get help.

It is much healthier to spank a child than to scream and nag him/her. A bruise on the bottom is much better than a bruise in the mind.

When your child knows you mean business, you will rarely have to correct them. You are the reason you are having trouble correcting them. If they actually have a "bad attitude" in their system, take him/her to your pastor or CHRISTIAN counselor. NO secular counselors. Don't just keep hollering at them. That will do neither of you any good.

Proverbs 22:15, *"Foolishness is bound in the heart of a child; but the rod (scion) of correction shall drive it far from him."*

Proverbs 23:13-14, *"Withhold not correction from the child; for if thou corrects him with the rod (scion) he shall not die. And YOU shall deliver his soul from   Hell."*

Proverbs 29:15, *"The rod (scion) and reproof give wisdom: but a child left to himself brings his mother to shame."*

It's pretty clear, God's Word says if we love our children we will correct them. It also says that you are shameful if you do not.

Are you a shame in Gods eyes? Are you one of the uninformed parents that say you shouldn't correct your kids? That means that you do not believe in the Bible, the absolute authority.

God initiated corporal punishment. Let me repeat myself again, there is A BIG DIFFERENCE in correcting a child and child abuse. One or two swats on the back side where God put the extra padding will usually do the trick. But if you feel like striking them over and over, and places other than their extra-padded rumps, you have an anger problem. Seek help before you hurt one of these little ones. THEY BELONG TO GOD – not you!!! You might be abusing God's property, and it is a fearful and terrifying thing to fall into the hands of the living God (Hebrews 10:31).

<u>Never, ever, ever, ever – correct your child when you are angry. If they need correction, it can wait until YOU cool down.</u>

6) *"But* they are bigger than me."

The straw broom can be an equalizer, even for teenagers.

7) *"But* they won't love me."

You cannot have love without respect. If they say they don't love you, that's a form of getting you back under control, and it obviously works.

8) *"But* I'm so busy when I get home."

Doing what? Too busy to train your children? Where are your priorities? You don't have to call that friend to see how their day went, or answer your texts. They can wait! Your children COME FIRST, they've waited all day for you.

9) *"But* my children are so young."

Even toddlers should be given a job. My daughter and I started making her bed when she was two years old. It was a game. It wasn't perfect. I never complained. ONLY JESUS CHRIST DID THINGS PERFECTLY. Do NOT give them a job that is overwhelming; or you will break their spirits, and that puts you at odds with God. Stop complaining. Make work enjoyable; it lasts a lifetime. Complainers are idiots! God hates grumbling and murmuring:

> Philippians 2:14-15, *"Do all thing without murmuring, that you may be blameless before God."*

> First Corinthians 10:10, *"Do not be a murmurer or GOD will destroy you."*

Got that? God hates murmuring. God is called the Destroyer in the Bible – are YOU on His Hit List?

10) *"But* my kids grumble so much that it's just easier and faster to do it myself."

The kids know that!!!

11) *"But* my kids refuse to do anything but be a couch potato."

Remove the electric cord from the television, and lock it in the trunk of your vehicle. Confiscate the cell-phone. They should have time limits on the cell anyway. It is extremely unwise for a parent to give free access to a cell phone. If they have a rebellion problem from the confiscation of their cell…stop the service. Be the adult and in charge. Also, parents MUST monitor their cell phones. It is NOT an invasion of privacy it is your responsibility to know what is going on with them. You are the adult. It is a way to be sure they are on the right tract. They are YOUR kids, and YOU are paying for the cell, so YOU own it…not them.

12)   *"But* my child won't listen to me; he/she goes to their room, slams and locks their door."

Take the door off and put it in a garage, or a shed that is locked, along with their cell phone for a couple of weeks. Cell phones are great to bring an unruly child into line.

13)   *"But* my kid will hide in the bathroom with the door locked."

REFER TO ANSWER 12. *Take the locks off - or remove the whole door and put it in the shed with the bedroom door.* They'll have something new to think about…"what time can I safely go to the bathroom when no one is walking by?" After all, it is YOUR house, not theirs.

14)   *"But* my kids are forever arguing with me anytime I say anything."

You never argue with your kids! That gives them the upper hand. ARGUMENT IS THE EXCHANGE OF IGNORANCE! And if they can pull you into an argument…they have just proved you are ignorant. After they do what they are told, subjects can be discussed in a civilized manner. Yes, kids can be civilized when they know they have to be. If they get irate again, send them back to their 'door-less' room. (Review numbers 6 & 12.) Another good way to have a civilized discussion is to make them physically write down their opinions and questions. They'll be a lot shorter.

Please bury this in your mind: When you argue with your child(ren), you are giving them the upper hand. They become the voice of authority.

15) *"But* sometimes I get so frustrated with my kids I wish someone would just take them."

It's generally your own fault! You're not being the parent. You are their subject and they are training you…

16) *"But* my kids are already out of control!"

Time to pull the rug out from under them! It will be hard when you are already trained. Make up a list of "House Rules" and post them on a conspicuous door, like their bedroom, or on the bathroom mirror. If they tear it down, repost it again, and again, and again. Talk to your Pastor or Elder if you are a single parent. They can and should be an authority figure, but this depends on what the kids have observed in the way of your respect for the pastor or elder. Set each child up with an hour of pastoral counseling. Set yourself up with two hours.

This is going to be hard…expect it! First, firmly remove privileges from them until they become cooperative. Now, this will be very hard and you cannot say "no" one day and after tantrums and badgering give in! That mean they are still in control. Once you tell them something…don't wimp out. When they try badgering you, if they won't go to their bedroom, you go to your bathroom and lock the door. Take a book with you (Preferably these Buts...).

It's very important to start removing important privileges. Like first is their cell phone…that will usually get a real explosion. If they will not give it to you…stop the service on it. Stop all their receiving outside calls, even if you have to unplug and hide the phone.

Stop computer use…even if you have to take the cord off the back of it. This too will surely get an explosion. How YOU act toward their first explosions will tell how well you will be able carry out YOUR God given function of training your children.

Do they have to be somewhere at a certain time? If they haven't done what you have told them to do…they don't get to go, I don't care if it is a school or church function. The world will not end if they completely miss the meeting. This is a good moral awakening for these irate and uncontrollable kids. Do not do their laundry, their meals. Do NOT give them money for anything. Get that list made up of their chores they will be getting paid for. FREE MONEY STOPS. You do not get free money for doing nothing, and they shouldn't either…it teaches them to be lazy and leaches.

But, remember, you will initially get explosions…but stick to your guns if you are serious. It is important for their well-being, and growing into a well-balanced adult. Take time to train them. Stop being their trainee.

I heard a very wise preacher (Adrian Rogers) say, "We don't train our children. We do train our dogs. We tie up our dogs at night. We let our kids run free…" How have you let this get backward?

Your kids need a curfew: I suggest 9:00 p.m. on school nights – IF their homework is done. If not, they stay home, no matter what was on their schedule. They will usually only miss an important event once; then they will get their acts together. A twelve or thirteen-year old should never be out after 9 pm…unless you have taken them to an event and will be picking them up.

We have pre-teens doing graffiti and stealing things. Oh, don't say, "My kid would never do that." The other parents probably say the same thing. You don't know what he or she will do under peer pressure! <u>*The peer pressure from 'friends' is a lot more important to them than what YOU say*</u>. Most of the kids that get into trouble have parents that said that very same statement.

Besides, if they are out late it does affect their ability to concentrate on schoolwork, etc., so keep their curfew in spite of their persistence and resistance.

YOU BE THE PARENT, the authority. Be the one in control! *Curfews also help to stop teen sex and pregnancy. Would you rather deal with a mad kid - or a pregnant one?*

Try This

Repeat this phrase, mean it, and see how God moves!

Dear Lord,

I love you, and I need you.

Please come into my heart.

Forgive all my sins.

Bless my family and me,

My home, my finances,

And my friends.

Please!

In *Jesus*'s name,

Amen and Amen

Unholy Sex and Sin

There are many forms of unholy sex, and all sin is unholy. Some of these are sex without marriage, extra-marital affairs, homosexuality, bestiality, rape incest, child molestation, lying, stealing, gossip, backstabbing, murmuring, and complaining. ALL SINS.

There are many more sin categories, perhaps one in which you are currently in bondage to. But in this treatise, we are going to discuss sex and sin.

Are you aware of Matthew 24:51? *"And I (God) shall cut him asunder (into pieces), and appoint him or her their portion with the hypocrites; there shall be weeping and gnashing of teeth."* This is for heinous or atrocious sin.

What is a heinous or atrocious sin? It is one that our God is especially repulsed by, and is going to give special treatment to the perpetrator. He or she will be cut into pieces to endure forever the pain of being torn apart, as well as being in the place where your eyelids cannot blink because of the blistering and blazing heat. Not a nice picture, is it? (Think about the babies during an abortion; they are literally torn apart. Imagine the pain they DO feel when their little arms or legs are ripped right off their little bodies.)

Picture Hell as a volcano, and it might be easier for you to forsake sin. That's what Hell is, being thrown into the lake of lava from a volcano! You will be in too much distress to know anything about your flesh burning. When you hear people joke about all their friends being there, they are stupid! They will not be able to know or recognize anyone. There are no furnaces down there to 'stoke' – only the constant screaming awareness of being buried in the lava surrounding them - forever.

One of the heinous sins in the Bible is CHILD ABUSE, in any form, and that includes abortion!!

Matthew 18:6-7, *""But who shall offend one of the little ones it would be better for him that a millstone were hanged about his neck. Woe to that man or woman by whom the offense cometh!"*

They used to grind the grain with a big stone called a millstone. It weighed hundreds of pounds, and the horses pull it around a wheel to grind the wheat into a powder.

God hates child abuse, whether it is sexual, nutritional, violence, neglect, lack of teaching, or anything else you can name. And, yes, abortion as a heinous act of child abuse. God says that a child is a child from the moment of conception. It doesn't "all of a sudden" become alive… **Anything growing is alive.** Read Psalms 139 if you don't think that is a baby in the womb. God does not call 'it' a blob. Verse 13, *"You have covered me in my mother's womb."* Verse 16, *"Your eyes did see my substance, yet being unperfect; and in Your Book all my members were written, which in continuance were fashioned, when as yet there were none of them."* All the parts of that baby's body were inscribed from eternity. God made that baby, no matter how it came into being.

If you don't believe God, then you are not very bright or informed. God is our Creator, and He says when we begin our lives, and when they are to be ended. Yes, even ended. More and more people are accepting euthanasia. That's murder, just as abortion is murder!

God calls child abuse heinous, and other than God, our spouses, our children are to be foremost in our caring. This means before friends, jobs, self, or things. They are precious in His sight, and had well better be in yours also. It is a grievous mistake to hurt a child, *either inside or outside the womb!* They belong to God, not you, and abortion kills God's property.

How dare anyone set themselves up above the Lord God! That's a heinous crime, and it will be punished in the heinous way God speaks of. If you have already done this heinous thing, there is forgiveness if you sincerely ask God for it, but you can never do it again, because now you are informed. There does come a time when there is no more forgiveness for sin.

Hebrews 10:26, *"For if we sin willfully after that we have received the knowledge of the Truth, there remains no more Sacrifice for sins."* After reading this book, you cannot say you have not been informed! Your sins WILL send you to Hell!

Another heinous sin in God's eyes is homosexuality. God says that homosexuals should be stoned. God calls homosexuals an abomination. Stop calling them 'Gay', they are not gay, most are miserable and the suicide rate is exorbitant.

Leviticus 18:22, *"You shall not lie with mankind, as with womankind: it is an abomination."*

To you who say, "They can't help it." Stop! Consider this, if you love and believe in God, why would you believe that He would create anything just to condemn it to Hell?

Second Peter 3:9, *"The Lord is not willing that any should perish, but that all should come to repentance."* If you believe it is not a 'chosen lifestyle', then you are calling God a liar! Calling God a liar means you are not saved and have no part in God's Heaven.

Acts 5:3-4, *"Ananias, why has Satan filled Your heart to lie to the Holy Spirit? Why have you conceived this thing in your heart? You don't lie to men...but to God."*

God killed Ananias on the spot for lying to God. (The Holy Spirit IS God.)

Are YOU a False Teacher for supporting homosexuality and lesbianism? That's what God calls anyone who does. That's pretty dangerous territory. You had better get into God's Word with an open mind, asking the Holy Spirit to help you understand truth, or you will be damned to Hell.

Read Romans 1:25-28 to see what God thinks of false teachers. Socially marginalized minions are being culturally swayed into making bad decisions. The goal of the homosexual activists is not the "happiness" for their 'flock'...but a grab for political power. And, after they use the demented victims – they cast them away like the garbage they have made of them. "Gender reassignment" as they call it – is just a way of taking the minds of unstable people into a deep, psychological and physical chaos that they will probably never recover from. There does come a point of no return. It's a recipe to the malignancy desire to commit suicide.

Homosexuality and lesbianism are just propensities. People have many propensities, like a propensity to steal...it's still sin! A propensity to lie...it's still sin! A propensity to murder...it's still sin! People have a propensity to be gluttons...it's still sin! There are many propensities we see in our everyday lives...but if not controlled...they are sin! People must refrain from sin, and get their propensities under control. A propensity is not a sin...until it is acted upon!

Second Peter 2:10, *"Chiefly them who walk after the flesh – in the lust of uncleanliness – are speaking evil of dignities."* This is speaking of anyone supporting the homosexual lifestyle be telling lies to whitewash it. You are not saved if you support this abomination to God, and have no part in God's Heaven.

Tran-sexual's WILL stand before the Throne of God as HE made them, not as Society did.

Thousands have come out of this abomination lifestyle after they received Christ *Jesus*, and are now living a happy married life with children. More proof that this is just a choice – not a defect a we are told.

Now, perhaps you agree to this point that child abuse and homosexuality are heinous sins, but God also put to death those fornicating or committing adultery. If you are having sex outside of marriage, you are a fornicator, and it is unholy and SIN! There is no other word for it. *Flings are sins multiplied!* They are not only adulterous but they are fornications too. That's a double whammy of sin, and really heinous.

I repeat, if you are not married to the one you are having sex with, you are a fornicator and it is sin! Even if you are single and engaged…sex is still fornication, and not God-ordained. You cannot be a Christian and be committing fornication and adultery.

Saint John 14:15, *"If you love me, you will keep my Commandments."* Fornicating is not keeping God's Commandments. You are not saved if you continue in sin.

Living together and having sex outside of, or before marriage, is not keeping the Lord's commandment, meaning you do not have the Lord, and are not His! Scary huh? If you are in an unholy situation, STOP! Get out, get down on your knees, and ask God's forgiveness, and make things right. *You could die today!!!* Where will you spend eternity of because of your lust and non-commitment to God? Remember the volcano?

Young lady, young man, if you are having sex before marriage, stop! You are on a banana peel headed straight for that volcano: Hell. NO ONE TRULY LOVED SOMEONE AND PULLED HIM OR HER INTO IMMORALITY. Immorality can never be love. If he says, "Baby prove you love me…" He has just proven he doesn't love you. You are only a cow, and he wants free milk. Run. Run to someone who does loves you enough to keep your relationship pure, someone who is more concerned about your Soul going to eternal damnation than his selfish sexual lust.

Keep in mind that men date whores, but they marry pure ladies. If he 'gets you' before marriage…you will not be pure and your relationship doesn't stand much of a chance at succeeding.

There is forgiveness. But in order to get God's forgiveness, you must repent, and you must abstain from the evil of fornication and adultery. You must ask the Lord for forgiveness, and you must abstain from future sexual activity in that or any other satanic relationship. That's right, satanic; if it is not of God, it is of Satan. What if the Rapture/Resurrection were to happen today? Where will you spend eternity? In the volcano?

Only blasphemy of the Holy Spirit is unforgiveable. You can have forgiveness if you sincerely ask The Lord for it, and abstain from further fornication. Repent in Webster's Dictionary says, "To turn from sin, be sorry; and to dedicate oneself to the amendment of one's life."

God invented sex – surprise! – for married people to enjoy. But sex is for marriage only.

Hebrews 13:4, *"Marriage is honorable in all, and the bed undefiled: but whoremongers and adulterers God will judge."*

In immoral and adulterous relationships and incidents of rape, the one you are naked before will in time find you repulsive. Yes, even the rapists, after violating their victims, generally find their victims repulsive, and often murder them because of their repulsion. Almost all of YOU who are violating God's Law will be repulsive to your "partner" sooner or later. <u>Why do you think the divorce rate is so high?</u> This has been since the beginning of time. Why would you be so stupid and naïve as to think your relationship is any different? Why would a person buy a cow whose milk they can get free, without strings or obligations - while wondering how many have been able to get free milk from this cow... You'll do until the next good-looking cow comes along.

Men look for whores to fornicate with, but virgins to marry!

Doesn't that tell you something?

Sin always has its consequences. Distress and anguish will come upon you if you disobey God. Oftentimes, you will have to sin again to cover a prior sin. Take the sin of abortion; that's a heinous one. How often another sin must be committed to cover up that sin; lies to bosses, friends, families and even doctors and health-workers. Sin breeds sin. If you eat thee fruit of wrong devices, God says he will allow simpletons and fools to destroy themselves because they hate knowledge. God is not brutal - but He is holy and just.

Friends, sin is usually shared. It's easy to find someone to sin with. It's usually fun at the time. That extramarital affair, that youth sex relationship and experimenting, that homosexual abomination, that child abuse, that lie, those unlawful drugs – all shared experiences.

But sin's consequences are always endured alone! You will be alone in your sorrow. I know girls who mournfully agonize in the night over an abortion they have had – ALL ALONE – in their misery and in almost inconsolable grief. They are sincerely repentant. Truly, I say unto them, based on God's Word, "Your sincerity and sorrow has touched the heart of the Lord, your Creator. He has forgiven you. You are not alone, He is there with you right now. Now, you must forgive yourself. And that's the hard part. God forgives you, honey. You are forgiven. Your sin is now in God's Sea of forgetfulness. It will be remembered no more. YOU WILL NOT BE JUDGED ON THAT SIN; you are forgiven. You must believe that. Yes, you will see and hold your little baby in Heaven, and it will not know of any of your sins. In Heaven, only good things are remembered, nothing bad. You will have peace and forever be with your little one. Be at peace. God loves you very much. You are His baby, His little one. Let Him hold you close until you can hold your own little one. He is your peace; accept Him right now. He is your Father. Talk to Him as you would a loving earthly father. He will always listen. He knows everything about you already; your thoughts, your feelings, your desires, and your agonies. Talk to him openly and honestly. Getting all your hurt out will make you feel much better. He loves you so very much. Let Him hold you and comfort you. He does care.

"The same goes for you victims who have been dragged into the homosexual lifestyle. God loves you so much. You are His baby. He is aching for you to turn your eyes, thoughts and heart to Him. Just as you love something you make and don't want it to end up in a fire, He made you and doesn't want you to end up in Hell. God cannot look on sin, and He is not the author of confusion."

First Corinthians 14:33, *"For God is not the author of confusion, but of peace."*

You must take the steps to God to find peace and forgiveness it is there. *Jesus* Christ weeps for his lost sheep, even a single one. Repenting and turning your life over to the Lord will make even the angels rejoice with your Creator. (Hebrews 14:10.) You will find contentment and grace in God's love. He wants to hold you on His lap. You are already in His heart!

Are you the one who caused a marriage to go wrong? Were you hateful, angry, controlling, badging, badmouthing, accusing, nasty, overbearing or selfish? Did you, perhaps, even commit adultery? Is that person you loved finding solace in the arms of someone else? Sin will tear your heart out. Don't be a simpleton or a fool to self-destruct yourself; only you are going to answer for your actions on judgment day – all alone. Lying to your mate is sin! Bad-mouthing your mate is sin! Selfishness is a sin…a big one!!! Most marriages end because of selfishness on one or both sides. I, I, Me, Me, seems to be the rule of life anymore, and that's sin. If you don't put your mate's welfare before yours, you are sinning. When you marry for better or for worse, and you make most of the worse, that is sin.

Sin is NEVER God tempting you. That's a fallacy.

JAMES 1:13, *"Let no one say when he is tempted, I was tempted of God, for God cannot be tempted with evil, neither tempt He any man."*

If you are being tempted, it is not of God. It is SELF. No, Satan didn't make you do 'it'. Slewfoot cannot make you do anything. You sin on your own. No sin can come upon you except that God will provide a way of escape if you will look for it or take it.

First Corinthians 10:13, *"There has no temptation taken you but such as is common to man: but God is faithful, who will not suffer you to be tempted above that you are able; but will with the temptation also make a way to escape, that you may be able to bear it."*

God is watching you right now. When He sees you in temptation, He will make a way for you to escape…just ask Him.

So, don't even think of blaming anyone else for your actions, not even the evil one - Satan. YOU are responsible to God!

But to you who broke up your marriage, I say, God loves you still. He loves you so very much, now and forever. He will forgive you if you ask Him and forsake your selfish ways. He has missed you so much. Return to Him. He feels loneliness for you, just like you feel loneliness for those who are gone. He understands. He wants you to ask for forgiveness and then forgive yourself.

God has another mate for you, but you must be ready for that new person. You must have a clean heart and a clean lifestyle. Why would a just God bring a new and good person into your life only to have you be selfish and vicious again? He will not bring you anyone until you are ready. Call on His Name. He is waiting.

There are at least ten verses in the Bible that say if you fall back in sin, you were never saved. So, are you back in the sin you asked forgiveness for? Are you on thin ice because of your lust of lack of self-control? Are you fornicating? Any sex outside of marriage is fornication. Perhaps you need to re-evaluate your circumstances and repent.

Bear in mind this verse that I put in earlier in this message (Hebrews 10:26.).

God is not willing that any should perish, and YOU are your own jail keeper.

You are now informed!

Stop now! It will send your soul to Hell. And YOU could die today!!!

Remember the volcano.

VOLCANOES
Hell's Entrances???
What's the difference between Hell and Sheol???

Now this is one 'hotly' debated subject... If this deep thought of mine doesn't make you shudder clear to your toenails...you are already dead!!!

I will be giving the Bible translations, plus both *Webster's Dictionary* and *Winston's Dictionary*... And, you really need to check out everything I say. I'm an ardent Bible study student, and you need to be too. We are living in hard times, perhaps the time of 'Woes' just before the Rapture/Resurrection - in fact...it could happen today...before you finish reading this Treatise...

Many people – who don't really study the Bible – say the word 'Rapture' is not in the Bible...However, in the Greek *rapture* and *resurrection* have the same meaning. The Greek and Hebrew Texts uses two words for describing virtually the same thing.

Exanastasis – "rising from the dead."
Exanistemi – "to raise up and away."
Then we go to the secular dictionaries and see the synoptic descriptions.

Rapture: *Webster's Dictionary:* "Being carried away." *Winston's* – " Carrying a person from one place to another.

Resurrection: *Webster's* – "Rising from the dead – to rise again." *Winston's* – "Bring again into use – remove from the grave." Both of the words are talking about rising again – from the grave. We SHALL rise again when *Jesus* Christ comes back for us. We shall be removed from the grave that holds only our mortal bodies. We shall have life again…Praise The Lord!!!

Heaven and Hell are very real places – and we shall spend eternity in one or the other. <u>Death is not final – it is just the beginning of eternity.</u>

Brimstone: *Webster's Dictionary:* "Yellow Color Sulphur. The Hebrews called any substance that caught fire easily Sulphur or sulfur." Both are correct. *Winston's Dictionary:* "A yellow color of Sulphur or sulfur." The word brimstone is found in at least seven passages of the Old Testament: Genesis 19:24, Deuteronomy 29:23, Job 18:15b, Psalms 11:6, Isaiah 30:33 and 34:9, and Ezekiel 38:22. Also in seven passages in the New Testament: Luke 17:29, Revelation 9:17 9:18, 14:10, 19:20, 20:10, and 21:8. It is used in Revelation as the symbol of the firey wrath of God and the future suffering of the wicked.

Sulfuros or Sulphuros (same meaning) *Webster's Dictionary:* "Of, relating to, or dealing with the fire of Hell. Burning Sulphur. Scathing. Virulent. Profane. Blasphemous." Mixtures of Sulphur and oil were used to set besieged cities on fire. They would use a catapult to fling the firey stones into the city. They would also catapult decaying animals or diseased bodies into a city to start epidemics among the population. This may well have been the earliest form of germ-warfare. From about 800 BC to AD 1500, the catapults were the most formidable weapons in the world.

However, they became obsolete when the much more maneuverable and accurate cannons came into being. Cannons could be moved much more readily and were easier to hide. Some of the large catapults would weigh several tons and throw a distance up to about 850 yards. The Roman armies were the ones who were most feared as to catapults. Winston's Dictionary: "Used in the manufacture of gunpowder and sulfuric acid, also called brimstone.

Molten *Webster's Dictionary:* "Fused or liquefied by heat." *Winston's Dictionary:* "Melted."

Volcano *Webster's Dictionary:* "A vent in the earth's crust from which molten or hot rock and acrid steam issues." *Winston's Dictionary:* "An opening in the earth's surface, generally surrounded by a mass of ejected material forming a more or less conical hill or mountain. Violent. Powerful. Explosive.

Inferno *Webster's Dictionary*: "Of or relating to Hell. Infernal in French means Hell. Hellish. Diabolical. Damned." Winston's Dictionary: "Situated below. The lower regions. Hell. A scene so horrible as to resemble Hell."

The first volcanic eruption for which a date can actually be estimated was 1694. It occurred at Cinder Cone, in the Lassen Peak district of California. That certainly wasn't the very first volcano, only the first that an actual date can be scribed. That was after Christopher Columbus discovered America in 1492. Incidentally, Christopher Columbus was a Christian, even though the revisionists are trying to write him out of the books as one, as well as make him a villain. He was not a villain, and he was a Christian.

Remember how, in the 'very olden days', people were cast into a volcano as a human sacrifice? These sacrifices were made to appease their gods. How utterly stupid can/could people be?

Could the volcanoes be the entrance to the lake of fire? Ever thought about that? Volcanoes are bottomless pits. Can you imagine being thrown into one? Every liquid in your body would immediately dry up. You wouldn't be able to blink again. Think about never being able to blink again. Try to keep from blinking for a, moment; your eyes get scratchy real fast. You wouldn't be able to see ever again.

You would stay conscious, but you wouldn't know what was going on around you. All you would hear would be the terrifying screams of others in their lava coffins.

Your mouth would be so dry that your tongues would stick to the roof of your mouth. You wouldn't be able to swallow – but don't worry about that – there would be no saliva to lubricate you anyway.

Your ears would no longer have the moist earwax. They would just be dry, with screeching pain from the screams of others around you – any yourself.

The sulfur fumes are very acrid; they are not only sharp and bitter to your tongue and nostrils, but they are pungent, burning and very irritating to the skin and tissues. Acrid fumes will burn lungs, so breathing would become almost impossible. Your body would be in a constant state of disintegration – all this forever and ever.
Matthew 24:51, "And The Lord shall cut him asunder and appoint him his portion with the hypocrites." Do you understand what we are told here? That means cut into pieces. Can you imagine being in a volcano lava coffin, all cut into pieces? We really cannot even comprehend that; it's too horrific for our minds to even conceive.

The time we spend on earth, some sixty to ninety years average, is only a dot in forever. Put a small dot on a piece of typing paper. See how much it covers? Not much. Now multiply this by trillions. That's your life here on earth compared to eternity.

If you are struggling here on earth, and people, spouses, grown children, or young children have got you down and depressed, think about your eternity. This life you are in right now may not be wonderful, and it may seem awful. But you had better press on toward the mark for the prize of the high calling of God in Christ *Jesus*. Paul tells us that in Philippians 3:14. And, Paul was in prison at that time. He certainly wasn't having an easy life.

God didn't say it would be an easy life for us here on earth. He did say He would be with us through whatever we have to go through. Satan has control of the air around us now. Blame him for all the junk in your way, at least the part he has thrown at you. However, YOU create a lot of your own 'junk' by making unwise decisions and actions.

The Bible says several times that if you don't follow Christ's Commandments, you are going to Hell! Reread the commandments. It is not a suggestion. It is a 'commandment' and YOU will ultimately decide where you will spend eternity. You can either spend it in a lava coffin in a volcano lake of fire, or in a heavenly mansion. You CAN resist the devil, and he will flee from you.

James 4:7-8, *"Submit yourselves therefore to God. Resist the Devil and he will flee from you. Draw near to God, and He will draw near to you. Cleanse your hands, you sinners; and purify your hearts, you doubleminded."*

Remember Sodom and Gomorrah? God rained down fire and brimstone from Heaven for their evil acts. Read Genesis 9, as it explains how God uses these elements for judgment and punishment. God used weather and elements forty-one times in the Bible for judgment, why would anyone think He will not use them again? What about the huge increase in earthquakes, floods and hurricanes? Are these, perhaps, God's judgments coming down on the earth for the evil that is so widespread now?

Sure, God is a loving God, not willing that any should perish, but God is a Holy and Righteous God. Many will perish because of their own sin, not because of God's Will.

Let's take a look at the different terms used in the Bible for the places wicked people inhabit.

SHEOL

This term is used sixty-five times in the Old Testament. Almost half of the 65 uses – 31 – are speaking of the "grave." This is where the body stays dead until the Lord returns, and you receive your glorified body. Your soul and spirit have already gone to either Heaven or Hades. There is no in between…the moment you die on earth, your soul and spirit are immediately transmitted to Heaven or Hell.

Paradise existed before the Cross. But when Christ went down into Hell while on the Cross, he emptied and closed Paradise. There is no such place in the Bible as a "Paradise" after the cross of Christ, where your soul and spirit await to be resurrected, or, as some mistakenly think, be bought out with money. It just doesn't exist anymore. That's a false teaching. The body remains in the 'grave.'

I hear people say, "But what about the thief on the cross? *Jesus* told him he would be in Paradise with him that very day?" That is misinterpreted lots of times. It doesn't matter if the body has been cremated, drowned, or dismembered, it will rise in tact when *Jesus* Christ calls it to Him.

Luke 23:43, *"And Jesus said unto him, Verily I say unto you, Today you shall be with me in Paradise."* (Greek, *paradelsos* = A Park, an Eden, a place to wait for future happiness.)

Jesus took the thief to Paradise with Him while He emptied it of all the saints of the Old Testament, that followed God before the cross. The thief accompanied Christ to Heaven along with all the Saints. Paradise was closed…to be no more.

HADES

This is the abode of the unsaved while they are awaiting the Great White Throne Judgment. In most instances in the Bible it is referred to as Hell. It is a place of terror for the souls and spirits who died '**unsaved**' and it is ruled by the demon gods of the underworld. It is the holding place for the souls and spirits awaiting judgment and eternal punishment in the Lake of Fire. Luke 16:23.

Christians will stand at the *Judgment Seat of Christ* – to receive their awards for what they did for HIM after they truly gave their lives to Him.

The unsaved are the ones who will stand at the Great White Throne, before God, to have all their sins made 'public' – and then be thrown into the Lake of Fire.

TARTARUS

This word in Greek is found only one time in the Bible. SECOND PETER 2:4, *"For if God spared not the Angels (Aggelos) who sinned, but cast them down to Hell (Tartarus in Greek), and delivered them into chains of darkness, to be reserved until judgment.)"*

It is a deep abyss, far below Hades. It is the lowest Hell.

During the time when *Jesus* was on the Cross, and He went down to Hell to free the Saints, He also preached to these fallen Angels. Some say the preaching was to the human spirits – but the Greek clearly calls these spirits *"aggelos"* which means an angel or messenger. These are the fallen Angels who tried to corrupt the human race, and are the ones that cohabitated with women, are still locked up in Tartarus. The Bible doesn't say whether these fallen Angels will be released when Satan comes back to rule for a short time or not. These wicked angels will ultimately stand before the Great White Throne and thrown into the Lake of Fire, along with Satan himself. This release of Satan, for a spell, happens after the Millennium reign of Christ *Jesus* on the earth.

GEHENNA

This word Gehenna is used 12 times in the New Testament. Greek has "geenna, and Hebrew calls it "gehinnom." It in its Greek annunciation text of 'yeevvav' it means "Valley of Hennon" or "Valley of doom." In the Hebrew 'era' it was where the fires burned the garbage of Jerusalem, which shows us a picture of the eternal fires of eternal doom for anyone not saved. The bodies of criminals and the destitute, along with the garbage, were thrown into this perpetual fire. Just like the fire of Hell will be perpetual. Hence, a place of burning or torment: Hell. Hell is real!

Your actions will send you to Hell! It's appalling when someone says, "I can't help it, I was born this way." That's a cop-out. It's poppycock, hogwash and a huge lie straight from the pit of Hell. Many people have a propensity and natural tendency or inclination to do something. We are born with a "sin nature" (thanks Adam and Eve), but we can control it. What about murder? There are those who have a propensity to murder; it's still a crime and sin! What about lying? Many people, alas, have a problem with telling the truth. People flippantly call them "habitual liars." The Bible says that the truth is not in them; it's sin. Drinking is a propensity – it's not right; it kills the mind and body – and often other innocent victims. It's SIN!

If anyone cannot control his or her propensity to do something evil, there is help in Heaven and in the earth. Don't go to a secular trained person; get to a Bible-trained and believing person who really cares about your soul and will tell you the truth. They just prescribe medication for you. Medication will not cure SIN. Evil is evil, and you can control it – if you stop listening to people who say you are just a victim of a horrible and ravaging disease.

I don't care where you came from, nor who your parents are, or how bad they were/are, nor what your surroundings were growing up, nor what has been done to you in secret. You can still have control over any propensity for evil that has 'victimized' you. Just don't do 'it'!

When *Jesus* Christ sets us free, we are free indeed. There is power in just saying His Name. "*Jesus, Jesus, Jesus,* please cover me with your blood, and help me do what is right." Don't let anyone push you into the 'victim mentality' and gain control over you. You belong to God, not the world.

The Global Volcanism Program at this time lists 12,887 Volcanos worldwide in the last 10,000 years, according to the Smithsonian Institute. God has lots of entrances to Hell to throw the unsaved. Agonizing cannot even begin to describe the condition - forever!

I would rather scare you into Heaven, than see you go to Hell.
Am I your enemy because I tell you the Truth???
<u>THINK ABOUT THE VOLCANO!!!</u>

What Color is Your Brain???

I was a medical secretary for about fourteen years (in my younger days) and worked for the hospital Pathologist mostly. I was a good typist back then, and Dr. Kelley had set me up a desk just outside the Morgue…so I could type the Autopsy reports as she related them to me during the procedures. She was a brilliant lady, and I have a great deal of respect for her still. She was truly informed in anatomy and detailed examinations. Some of this information comes from her, she was a walking encyclopedia.

The mass of tissue you have in your skull can be held in your two hands. This three – to four-pound object has a storage capacity of more than two quintillion bits. That is a 2 followed by thirty-six zeroes, so says the *Table of Numerology* in *Webster's Dictionary*.

It is also said that you or I can store in our brains twenty thousand times the information contained in the complete *Encyclopedia Britannica*. Just image for a moment the weight of what our brains can store. I don't know of anything that could lift our consolidated knowledge. There are enormous cranes that can lift things of great size. But if everything in your brain were brought to stature development, wow, it would be amazing in size. Let your mind wonder a bit and try to visualize your brain's storage area.

I have heard, based on research, that when we use some of our brain cells they become a different color than the ones we don't use. Scientists also say that on an average we only use about five-percent of the capacity of our brain. That's a real shame. What have we not done that we might have? Even considering just five-percent of two quintillion, that is a lot of storage bits. But thinking about the other 95 percent the average person doesn't use – won't put to work – I sometimes think How awful!

I ponder what changes each of us could affect in the world for good if we were not so lazy. What if we were to use 10-percent of our brains? We are our only limitations. Reading is a key factor. Exercise your brain. Pump, pump, pump.

It is possible during an autopsy to determine approximately how much of the brain the deceased had used during the time he or she lived. Just like the quail, our brain cells begin as white meat. So, until you exercise your brain…it stays one color: white.

The unexercised portions of most animals and birds have different colors in their meat. The white meat is the unexercised portion, such as the breast. The darker meat, such as legs and thighs, are parts of the animal that to the work. However, the dove is all dark meat, a little worker. How is your flesh?

Consider this. It will give you perspective. Say you own a 100-unit apartment building. But there is only 5-percent of it rented. That's 95 percent unoccupied. With all those unoccupied apartments, you wouldn't be able to make your utility and tax payments. You would be very discouraged and would certainly do something to upgrade your percentages to a positive.

So, why don't you upgrade your brain? It's the same idea. You have an imagination. Use it. READ, READ, READ. Devote a little time every day to study, preferably the Bible. It will discolor your brain!

Common sense dictates that you should always have an ace in the hole, a plan-B if plan-A doesn't work. You should not go off the deep end if something goes wrong. *They always will!!!* Just be sure and have a Plan-B or C or D in the vast, unused storage area of your brain. Use your brain cells…discolor them. I'm constantly in the process of trying to discolor my brain.

If you are failing – you either lack guts or discolored brain cells. Get off your lazy – poor little me - fanny and get busy on another Plan!

2,000,000,000,000,000,000,000,000,000,000
Sure – it just evolved! And pink pigs fly…

YOU ARE RESPONSIBLE

Don't give the responsibility of yourself
to somebody else
<u>You</u> are responsible.
Don't try to blame someone else for
your circumstances.
<u>You</u> are responsible.
Don't blame anyone else for
your behavior.
<u>You</u> are responsible.
Don't force others to make your
decisions for you.
<u>You</u> are responsible.
Don't despise others for your lack
of wisdom in stewardship.
<u>You</u> are responsible.
<u>You are responsible - to God!</u>

THOUGHTS APLENTY

MARIE GRACE

www.ingramcontent.com/pod-product-compliance
Lightning Source LLC
Chambersburg PA
CBHW071607080526
44588CB00010B/1049